Emerging Voices

Emerging Voices

Helping College Students
Reclaim Christian Proclamation

Barry L. Saylor

Foreword by Paul R. Alexander

WIPF *&* STOCK · Eugene, Oregon

EMERGING VOICES
Helping College Students Reclaim Christian Proclamation

Copyright © 2020 Barry L. Saylor. All rights reserved. Except for brief quotations in critical publications or reviews, no part of this book may be reproduced in any manner without prior written permission from the publisher. Write: Permissions, Wipf and Stock Publishers, 199 W. 8th Ave., Suite 3, Eugene, OR 97401.

Wipf & Stock
An Imprint of Wipf and Stock Publishers
199 W. 8th Ave., Suite 3
Eugene, OR 97401

www.wipfandstock.com

PAPERBACK ISBN: 978-1-7252-6368-0
HARDCOVER ISBN: 978-1-7252-6361-1
EBOOK ISBN: 978-1-7252-6362-8

Manufactured in the U.S.A. 10/30/20

This book is dedicated to my wife, Jess. Throughout this project you have served faithfully as my chief editor and encourager. Thank you for believing in me and in this project.
Romans 12:10b

For last year's words belong to last year's language.
And next year's words await another voice.

—T. S. ELIOT

You then, my child, be strengthened by the grace that is in Christ Jesus, and what you have heard from me in the presence of many witnesses entrust to faithful men who will be able to teach others also.

—2 TIMOTHY 2:1–2 (ESV)

Contents

Foreword by Paul R. Alexander | ix
Acknowledgements | xi

Introduction | 1
1. It's Time to Talk About Talking About Faith | 7
2. Secularism and the Twenty-First Century Emerging Adult | 22
3. A Collegial Response | 34
4. Screens Disciple | 46
5. An Analog Response | 60
6. Exiles in Training | 69
7. Interview Methodology | 93
8. In Their Own Words | 102
9. Keep the Conversation Going | 118

Bibliography | 127

Foreword

HUMAN SOCIETY HAS ALWAYS recognized different generations. Ancient cultures were often quite particular in providing rites of passage from one stage of life to another. This is very obviously evident in ancient Jewish society where the transition from childhood to adulthood is celebrated in a very deliberate way.

In the past two decades technological advances and globalization have been forces that have led to the defining of generational responses and the subcultural expressions of different age groups. Much of the emphasis on generational differences has been driven by marketing experts but has also found its way into the social sciences. Social analysts, educators and fashion businesses have found it useful to define generational traits and cater to them. Christian leaders have, likewise, recognized the specific generational needs of young people attending their services and have structured programs in response.

This book is helpful in navigating this obsession on generational differences in several ways. Firstly, it is clearly well researched and scholarly. It is readable and practical but has been carefully written taking credible research into consideration. Secondly, it has the authentic tone of a practitioner. This is not a volume that proposes mere theory. It is grounded in the life experience of the author and is thus of great value to the reader. Finally, it is clearly spiritual. By this I mean that the intent to equip the reader to reach a section of our youth with the love of Christ is front and center. These strengths combine to make this volume a very commendable addition to the literature on ministry to emerging generations.

I commend this book. It is ideal as a text for those who work in ministry preparation. It is a treasure trove for those actively involved in ministry to emerging generations. It is a gift to parents navigating the challenging process of raising well-adjusted young people. It is useful for small groups

Foreword

and discussion circles. In short it is a valuable addition to any reading list. My only advice is to not discount any of the book. Dive deep, read carefully and learn well. Ultimately, be sure to love young people because of their intrinsic value to their creator.

It seems to me that many are looking for the next "killer app" or short cut to success. Simply, it does not exist. Young people need respect, care and understanding. This book will be a great help to those who understand this and are prepared to make the sacrifices necessary to win young people to Christ and disciple them effectively.

Paul R Alexander, PhD
President, Trinity Bible College and Graduate School
Ellendale, ND

Acknowledgements

This project would not have been possible without contributions from a wealth of people who recognized its potential. First, I want to thank the students who allowed me into their lives during the fall 2018 semester at Trinity Bible College and Graduate School. Spending time with you throughout my doctoral research, on which this project is based, was a continual reminder of the passion behind the work. Thank you for your time and your willingness to share.

Secondly, I want to thank my doctoral committee. Susan Reese, I am grateful for every challenge and encouragement that you provided. I vividly remember our first conversation regarding this project and how your enthusiasm gave me confidence that I was moving in the right direction. Thank you for all you have done for me, both throughout this project and beyond.

Larry Caldwell, your words at the end of my defense helped me to see this project as something with more potential than I had imagined. Thank you for your direction then and after, as I have worked toward publishing my work.

Paul Alexander, I appreciate your willingness to push me to be better than the requirements of the assignment. This challenge has given life to my study and has pushed me to seek further engagement.

Carol Alexander, I am so thankful for your knowledge in contemporary culture and the changing role of the theological campus within this context. Time and again you directed me toward a resource that assisted in my research and broadened my understanding.

This project would not have been possible without the most important member of my doctoral team: my wife, Jess. You have served as my chief editor, proofreader, reading partner and of course, consulting therapist throughout this project. More than anyone else, this could not have happened without you. Beyond the hours of reading, listening and engaging

Acknowledgements

my topic, you believed in this project—and in me—before I did. You will always be my favorite conversation partner and this project is significantly better because of you. Thank you for all you have done, and for never allowing me to give up because you believed I had something valuable to say.

To Peyton and Olivia: We did it! Dad's book is finished! Thank you for giving up evenings and weekends each time I was pushing to finish a chapter, for celebrating every mile marker in a way that only you can, and for inspiring me to become a better scholar, and a better father. You are a daily reminder of my passion for emerging generations, and I am so proud to be your dad!

Thank you also to my parents and my older brother who have stood behind me every step of the way. You have been with me through both good and difficult times and I will always be proud to be a Saylor. Through life's challenges we have seen God's faithfulness and discovered more about His character.

Lastly, I would like to thank Trinity Bible College and Graduate School for graciously facilitating this study. Whether with students in class, or with staff and faculty at coffee, this study quickly became a living, breathing organism which many of you endured throughout its development. I am thankful to have been able to process ideas with a collegial staff and faculty. This is a special environment and I cannot imagine a better place to have landed for this study. This work will always follow me, both in what has been done and in the exceptionality of the environment in which it was completed.

Introduction

ANYTIME ONE ATTEMPTS A generational study of sorts, there is the danger of speaking about another generation in a way that is not constructive. A recent social media exchange comes to mind. At a time when poking fun of Millennials was at its height, the Twitter hashtag #HowToConfuseAMillennial was launched and, as social media often does, the multitudes responded in mass. Below are some examples of the first wave of content:[1]

- Show them a phone book. *#HowToConfuseAMillennial*
- Turn off their autocorrect. *#HowToConfuseAMillennial*
- Hand them a job application form. *#HowToConfuseAMillennial*

But then a funny thing happened; these young people turned the tables, sharing what they find confusing, and even condemning, about the choices they face in contemporary society:

- Destroy the housing market. Replace grad jobs with unpaid internships. Tell them to buy a house. *#HowToConfuseAMillennial*
- Crash their economy and then condescendingly ask why so many of them are living with their parents. *#HowToConfuseAMillennial*
- Tell them to follow their passions! As long as they aren't passionate about art, writing, or anything creative. *#HowToConfuseAMillennial*
- Baby Boomers will tweet *#HowToConfuseAMillennial* then call us to fix their internet problems 30 seconds later.

---

1. Listed tweets were taken from Powell and Argue, *Growing With*, 19–20. More samples from this exchange can be found at https://twitter.com/hashtag/howtoconfuseamillennial.

Now, before this text devolves into its own unhelpful version of generational punditry, it is important to identify a kingdom problem in this social media altercation. What is apparent in all of these tweets? Each of them points the finger at *another* instead of identifying bonds that should unify, and in doing so these generations of "tweeters" might have missed an opportunity to learn from one another and, hypothetically speaking of the church, for the kingdom of God to be advanced.

A Bold New World

I would propose that the emerging generation of students in our Christian colleges and universities is attempting to teach us something about reaching their generation, perhaps even pointing inadvertently to some level of what the new normal of church ministry might be following the tumultuous times in which they live. It is up to those in Christian higher education to handle this transition with wisdom and grace and to seek to understand how best to speak the language of these emerging generations in our theology and in training church leaders prepared to impact the world.

In their book *Faith for Exiles*, David Kinnaman and Mark Matlock contended that many in Western Christianity are attempting to prepare young people for a culture more closely resembling the world from which adults have come than the one in which young people currently live. In their words: "We believe many parents, educators, pastors, and other leaders are trying to prepare young Christians for Jerusalem, to keep them safe and well protected for a world they no longer live in."[2] This project seeks to understand the cultural challenges of the world in which today's emerging adult lives and to fashion a response by which theological education equips young Christian leaders to proclaim their faith in their world.[3]

The Failed Secular Experiment

The secular world of the twenty first century is a world that has lost the enchantment of the ages. Mark Sayers, pastor of Red Church in Melbourne,

---

2. Kinnaman and Matlock, *Faith for Exiles*, 28.

3. This point is also made in the words of Nicholas Fury beginning at 17:42 of *Captain America: The Winter Soldier*: "Shield takes the world as it is, not as we like it to be." Anthony Russo and Joe Russo, dir., *Captain America: The Winter Soldier* (2014, Hollywood, CA, Marvel Studios, 2014), Film.

Introduction

Australia, calls it the "soft power" of a post-Christian culture: "They don't bludgeon you out of your faith; they subtly coax you, each option quietly proclaiming a kind of gospel in itself, in which the good life can be yours."[4] And yet this "godless utopia" that the secularists had promised is anything but. In the midst of the failed secular experiment stands a God of order and of peace and of justice; a God who transforms lives and communities. And in the midst of this world seemingly devoid of hope stands a generation yearning for reform; eager for supernatural transformation.[5] Theological higher education, then, must accept the call to raise up leaders equipped to proclaim the gospel in their world.

Technologically Incapacitated

It also cannot be denied that technology has influenced the way today's emerging adults communicate. Think of the communication innovations that have come about in the lifetime of the average emerging adult: the iPhone, Facebook, Twitter, Instagram Snapchat, YouTube, blogging sites and texting that have moved communication from voice to text, video chat and conferencing, and many more. Technology has drastically changed the way emerging adults communicate.

While many of these innovations provide new opportunities for connection, research demonstrates that they also come with serious challenges. Emerging adults are affected internally by technology's constant presence through their loss of authentic community and increased anxiety. Externally, they are exposed to a more personalized view of the world through the attempts of media and tech giants who seek to capture their attention

---

4. Sayers, *Disappearing Church*, 10–11.

5. Keep in mind that the current generation of college and university students have experienced quite a tumultuous period, particularly in American history. Many of these students were born around the time of the Enron scandal, were learning to walk and talk at the time of the dot-com bust of 2000, survived the terrorist attacks of September 11, 2001, were beginning to form a worldview around the time of the 2008 financial crisis, and are now entering their vocational training and/or career in the uncertain environment caused by the outbreak of COVID-19. Not only is this generation hungry for transformation, but they have been uniquely conditioned to be one's to lead in this endeavor. This generation's circumstances have forced them to develop a level of toughness which caused one book to predict that these students "will have a strong work ethic similar to Baby Boomers and the responsibility and resiliency of their Generation X parents." Seemiller and Grace, *Generation Z Goes to College*, 7.

and dollars. They are also lured into a sentimental sort of online activism that often falls short of its intended goals.

These realities add up to a particularly threatening environment in which to empower emerging adults to proclaim their faith. Again, this is a reminder that theological education must speak to the world in which emerging adults live, especially when it comes to encouraging the proclamation of their faith.

Missional Togetherness

Once one recognizes the challenges set before this generation, and specifically how this is limiting one's Christian proclamation, it is imperative for the theological institutes of higher education to attempt to envision a better way forward. The community of the college or university campus has long been a formational body that facilitates this kind of development, and thus community must be at the heart of any response. Recent research suggests, however, that younger generations in North America are less trusting of the foundational components of this community. The Pew Research Center noted that American adults ages 18–29 "stand out for their comparatively low levels of trust" when it comes to confidence in both individuals and key institutions.[6] The very idea of community, which was once based on one's neighbors and institutions, has been diminished, and theological campuses are not immune to this reality.

In order to raise up proclaimers of the gospel it is important that our campus communities not only be relationally intentional, but that they also be missionally intentional. This means that young people ought to experience a sense of belonging and identity as they disengage from contemporary culture, but also that they ought to be dared to take a missional posture as their campus experience challenges them to reengage with a culture increasingly unfriendly to their Christian values.

A Messianic Deconstruction

Research suggests that today's emerging adults already seek this kind of missional stance. Two Dutch cultural theorists recently addressed this

---

6. Gramlich. "Young Americans are less trusting of other people—and key institutions—than their elders."

issue, proclaiming that postmodern irony and cynicism have been replaced with what they are calling a "new sincerity." This new stance "still wants to deconstruct, but not wantonly. Rather, by deconstructing beliefs, conventions, and traditions, it believes it can create a better world. It is cultural deconstruction with a messianic purpose. It believes we can have a better world, but it is not sure how to get there."[7] This messianic deconstructionism is a reminder of the hope this emerging generation represents even as one examines the austerity of their condition.

An Empowered Generation

On May 7, 2012, the *Atlantic* published an article by Jen Doll titled, "On the Importance of Having superheroes." Doll reflects in the article on the cultural fascination in the U.S with superheroes. Based on the success of *The Avengers*, and other films in this genre, she says, "We want something bigger than us—these are like the steroid fables of our time, the giant, expansive, special-effects-laden lessons through which we can hope to look at humanity and do a little better in the human-world."[8] Such a fascination with superheroes betrays a longing for supernatural power to help overcome human limitations in real life. Doll concludes, "The beauty of superheroes is that they're aspirational while still at the same time relieving any pressure to actually become a superhero because, well, that's impossible."

Christians cannot rest easily in such a conclusion. Sharon Galgay Ketcham, in her book *Reciprocal Church*, says, "The Spirit's presence and the inconceivable go hand in hand."[9] Ketcham captures Theologian Wolfhart Pannenberg's portrayal of the Spirit's power as lifting us out of our limited selves and into a power that exceeds human ability. For when the Spirit is present, superhuman abilities are possible.

The central cultural challenge facing theological education is an attack on the very thing which will treat the wounds of our communities: the power of the Spirit. In spite of its quest for a secular reality apart from God, our world continues to thirst for the supernatural and to seek out something in which to believe. It is our task to raise up leaders who have intentionally disengaged from a failed secular agenda in order to identify with the power of the Spirit—the only power that can bring the hope the

---

7. Sayers, *Disappearing Church*, 38.
8. Doll, "On the Importance of Having Superheroes."
9. Ketcham, *Reciprocal Church*, 81–82.

world seeks. It is also the task of theological higher education to critically engage a generation that is facing challenges unlike those known in recent history. As one author wrote in his hypothetical commencement speech to the class of 2020:

> Fall to pieces. Delete your thesis.
> Break up the ships that chase golden fleeces.
> your pure imaginations
> will flight angelic wars
> as the talons of the sunset
> touch the socially distanced stars.
> Yours, all yours, is the future of America
> and its promise without measure.
> No pressure.[10]

Today's emerging adults are inheriting a world that needs the gospel as much as any time in American history, and yet the research indicates that young people are less prepared and likely to share their faith. What is it that has led to this predicament and what can theological institutions of higher education do to change this trajectory? This book seeks to answer these questions and, perhaps more importantly, inspire a conversation on faith language. If the church is to continue in its mission, then it is imperative that Christian colleges and universities empower today's emerging adults to proclaim their faith in the culture in which they are familiar. Only then can we claim to be preparing young people for *their* culture and only then can the church find hope that it will continue to speak to the American public.

---

10. Parker, "The Advice that Most 2020 Commencement Speakers Won't Give."

1

It's Time to Talk About Talking About Faith

IN THE PROLOGUE TO *Scholarship & Christian Faith: Enlarging the Conversation*, Rodney J. Sawatsky, former president of Messiah College, makes the statement, "Scholarship at its best is much more than the pursuit of truth: it is the quest for wisdom."[1] Although most in academia would agree with this statement, sociological research seems to indicate that something is amiss.[2] In my opinion, the contemporary worldview of American culture has inhibited this "quest for wisdom" especially in its devaluation of faith. This statement will be supported later as two major areas of influence in American culture are examined, specifically their effect on faith language. Our pursuit is to identify the theological campus' role in reclaiming the quest for wisdom, especially in reclaiming the Christian language in the preparation of young ministers. Specifically, this project will seek what the theological campus can do to reclaim the language which is at the core of one's Christian identity.[3] With this in

---

1. Jacobsen and Jacobsen, *Scholarship & Christian Faith*, 3.

2. Specifically, the National Study of Youth and Religion, along with its follow up research following students into emerging adulthood: Smith, *Soul Searching*, Smith, *Souls in Transition*, and Smith, *Lost in Transition*. Also, Arnett, *Emerging Adulthood*.

3. The connection between language and identity is documented widely, but this connection is put especially well in the words of Ruth Wodak: "Language and identity thus have a dialectic relationship. Languages and using language manifest 'who we are', and we define reality partly through our language and linguistic behavior." Wodak, "Language, Power, and Identity."

mind, we will attempt to measure the impact of American culture, how this has affected college students in theological institutions as they enter their studies and the role of the theological campus in reclaiming such an identity, specifically through a reclamation of the faith language.

The Underlying Question

There is an underlying question that lies behind this project. How does interaction among students, faculty, and staff on a theological campus affect students' ability to develop an aptitude to verbalize their faith? This question will first be informed by an extensive literature review, specifically focusing on the effect of contemporary culture. I will then propose a communal response on the theological campus which will seek to facilitate student growth in the area of faith proclamation. After reviewing the literature in these areas, I will present an empirical study from my doctoral research done on the campus of Trinity Bible College and Graduate School (TBCGS), where I serve as a professor.

Setting the GPS Coordinates

First, it is important to understand the effects of twenty-first-century culture on the average Christian student entering college. Nancy Pearcey, former Francis A. Schaeffer Scholar at the World Journalism Institute, notes the dichotomization of social life in the secular thinking of Western cultures such as the United States, which has effectively eliminated biblical wisdom from the equation.[4] Whether one considers this through the lens of Peter Berger's private versus public sphere[5] or Francis Schaeffer's upper and lower story,[6] religion has been relegated to a discussion of values or preferences rather than considered alongside areas of scientific knowledge.[7] Studies such as the National Study of Youth and Religion

---

4. Pearcey, *Total Truth*, 20.

5. Berger, *Facing Up to Modernity*, 133.

6. Francis A. Schaeffer's divided concept of the upper and lower story are addressed throughout both Schaeffer, *Escape from Reason*, and Schaeffer, *The God Who is There*.

7. Berger notes the danger of such a dichotomy: "The individual is left to his own devices in a wide range of activities that are crucial to the formation of a meaningful identity, from expressing his religious preference to settling on a sexual life style." Pearcey, *Total Truth*, 20.

(NSYR) and Jeffrey Jensen Arnett's examination of emerging adulthood demonstrate that the disconnect of faith is taking a toll on today's college-age young person,[8] providing tangible evidence that this marginalization has been detrimental.

Specifically, this study seeks to examine the loss of an ability to proclaim one's faith, a concern noted by researchers in the landmark NSYR. After interviewing over three thousand young people for this study, Christian Smith and his research team found the majority of young people to be "incredibly inarticulate" when it came to discussing their faith, religious beliefs and practices, and the meaning of these in their lives.[9] Many, when questioned on other matters, offered articulate and reasoned responses, while their answers to faith questions left them stuttering, stammering and offering non-statements regarding their faith. Smith said that it seemed that for many of the young people interviewed these were "the first time that any adult had ever asked them what they believed and how it mattered in their life."[10] Researchers concluded that these young people, who had displayed the ability to be quite conversant and coherent when speaking of issues such as the dangers of drug abuse and sexually transmitted diseases, had done so because they had been educated and had been challenged to converse in these areas, while religion seems to have never been addressed in this manner.

Smith proposes that young people might be much more conversant when it comes to their faith if they were simply taught the language.[11] Recognizing the divide that secularism has created between the public and the private sphere and in relegating religion to nothing more than a subjective discussion of personal values, this concern is more readily understandable. The areas in which students were conversant were areas more commonly recognized as scientific knowledge, as rational and verifiable information and identified as objectively important for young people to understand.[12] Knowledge of one's faith, however, has been relegated to the private sphere,

---

8. Results from each of these studies will be examined more closely below.
9. Smith, *Soul Searching*, 131.
10. Smith, *Soul Searching*, 133.
11. Smith, *Soul Searching*, 133.
12. Pearcey identifies this brand of thinking as the "Enlightenment Idol" in Pearcey, *Total Truth*, 38–39.

stories connect to the grand story of God.[16] However, an understanding of stories, or even a functional grasp of Christian vocabulary, is not enough to learn to speak Christian in the way of being able to *proclaim* one's faith. It is apparent in the reading of the NSYR that some in the study could have given informed accounts of biblical narratives or catechisms learned as children; however, being able to verbalize one's faith goes beyond a recognition of information. A proclamation of faith requires a personal connection, a story that is connected to God's story. This study will seek to pinpoint that connection: the integration between one's individual story and the grand story of God in history and in the biblical account.

The role of the theological campus in making this connection, then, is important to understand. For this study, the integrational model of higher education proposed by Arthur Holmes and Nicholas Wolterstorff in the mid-1970s will specifically be addressed. This model counters a secular view that marginalizes faith, instead recognizing faith as a valid conversation partner alongside of other areas of knowledge. Much of Christian higher education in the twenty first century is modeled after this approach to education. This study will seek to measure the impact of this integrational approach to theological higher education, especially regarding the language formation of ministry students.

Lastly, it is helpful to present an exilic model when considering the role of the theological campus, as an institutional stance against the marginalization of Christian faith and its place in public discourse. The metaphor of contemporary church as an exilic community has been widely trumpeted by Old Testament scholar Walter Brueggemann,[17] and has subsequently been taken up by others in his wake.[18] These scholars have recognized the shift in culture to where the church and its voice have been marginalized and have looked to the biblical exilic community in an attempt to apply such a model in maintaining—and perhaps reclaiming—the Christian identity of the church.

---

16. The "co-construction" of one's autobiographical memory as presented by Fioretti et al.. "The Role of the Listener on the Emotional Valence of Personal Memories in Emerging Adulthood" is in view here: "Co-construction deals with the fact that recalling a past event in a relational context can produce small and progressive changes in the nature of autobiographical knowledge due to the narrative interaction between speaker and listener."

17. First proposed in Brueggemann. *Cadences of Home*.

18. Included, but not limited to Frost. *Exiles*, *Exile: A Conversation with N.T. Wright*, ed. by Scott, and *Exilic Preaching*, ed. by Clarke.

as non-rational and non-cognitive preference rather than truth, making one's faith subjective and relative to particular faith groups.[13]

It is also notable that technology has greatly influenced communication in the contemporary age. This is not only apparent in the practical application of technology, but also in how these new tools have affected emerging adults both internally and externally.

Our first goal, then, will be to identify the influence that these cultural factors have had on the average incoming theological college student and their ability to verbalize their faith.

Secondly, we will seek to identify the role of the theological college in reclaiming the language of faith. Theological colleges seek to reverse the trends of studies like the NSYR by instilling language as a key characteristic of Christian identity in one's preparation for their vocational calling. Such development of a Christian language is recognized not only as an academic exercise, but as a factor in building Christian culture rather than capitulating to the contemporary version.

Stanley Hauerwas, in speaking at the Princeton Lectures on Youth, Church, and Culture in 2007, augments the conversation on just such a language: "I hope to show why learning to think, as well as learning a language constitutive of thinking, is rightly understood as work done with our hands."[14] Language, then, is an *activity* of Christianity; learning to "speak Christian" is not only informative but is formative. Instilling this language of faith thus serves as a cornerstone for the theological institution in setting itself apart as a "beginning of wisdom," as it instills an overwhelming awareness of God, His creation and one's identity from this standpoint. This study seeks to not only cement the connection between the impact of contemporary culture and the loss of Christian language in today's emerging adults, but also attempts to identify the role of the theological campus in reversing this trend, specifically in the training of emerging adults called into vocational ministry.[15]

Central to this tenet is that students are learning the stories of others—biblical and church historical figures—and how these and their own

---

13. The conclusions made in this paragraph will be fleshed out in more detail later.

14. Hauerwas, "Carving Stone, or, Learning to Speak Christian".

15. Hauerwas made this point when, in a commencement address for Eastern Mennonite Seminary in 2010, he said that all the reading they had and would continue to do throughout their theological education was for one purpose: "to learn to speak Christian." Hauerwas, *Working With Words*, 86.

Brueggemann's model seems suitable for understanding the theological student in twenty-first-century culture in that the exile finds themselves as a stranger in a strange land, as one whose language, tradition and religious belief leaves her marginalized from mainstream culture. Accordingly, we will look at theological students through this exilic lens to determine if this is a helpful model through which the theological campus ought to see its mission.

The challenge of the exilic community is to maintain one's identity in the midst of an unfriendly culture. As has been addressed briefly above and will be addressed more fully in a later chapter, the Christian emerging adult in twenty-first-century America finds themselves in just such a relationship to contemporary culture. Much of the church's ministry to youth has had to recalibrate itself, as research over the last decade and a half has demonstrated a failure in fostering a lifelong faith in emerging generations.[19] This refocusing has been adopted in an effort to maintain the Christian identity of a generation in spite of a culture that counters many of its most basic values and beliefs. At the core of these models lies the question, "To what degree will the church's teenagers spend the rest of their lives loving God, loving people, and *making disciples* of all peoples for the glory of God?"[20] As will become clear in the pages of this text, this is a question that continues into emerging adulthood which in many ways has extended the transition of adolescence into the late twenties. Such a question seeks not only a maintenance of communal involvement, but an impassioned identity that seeks to proliferate the faith. A question this pertinent in the church's attempt to reclaim Christian identity in its emerging generations is that much more important in training the young ministers who will set the course in correcting these issues in the decades to come.

In proposing the exilic metaphor, we will attempt to identify the role of the theological campus in solidifying students' faith identity and, more to the point, to understand how it can increase students' ability and

---

19. See a recent article by Richard Ross in the *Journal of Youth Ministry* that notes extensive research demonstrating that only about 10 percent of teenagers emerge from ministries as "believers who will, for a lifetime, love God, love people, and make disciples for the glory of God." Ross' model emphasizes youth ministry in thirds: nurturing deeper faith relationships with parents (or adoptive church parents), a more intentional connection to the wider church congregation, while maintaining a healthy connection to their peers. Ross, "Youth Ministry in Thirds." Other recent models that have attempted to address this concern including Clark, *Adoptive Youth Ministry,* and Powell et al., *Growing Young.*

20. Ross, "Youth Ministry in Thirds," emphasis added.

confidence in proclaiming the faith that is central to their identity. It is my hope that this exilic lens will provide definition to the role of the theological campus in this age and that this model will provide a useful framework for which to understand both the challenges and the opportunities presented in the contemporary context.

Testing the Data

In addition to the literature review of the first part of this book, an empirical qualitative study, done in the Fall of 2018 on the Bible college campus where I teach,[21] will help to further the discussion. TBCGS is a Pentecostal Bible college[22] affiliated with the Assemblies of God, where I serve as Associate Professor of Biblical and Theological Studies (Family Ministry).[23] The interviews done for this study were done with traditional undergraduate students in a variety of vocational ministry programs. (See Figure 1) This age group has received a great deal of attention as of late, as sociologists have recognized a lengthening of adolescent characteristics in American young people. In fact, this period of development has gained new characterization as "emerging adulthood" in academic circles over the past decade

---

21. https://trinitybiblecollege.edu Trinity Bible College and Graduate School is located in Ellendale, ND, is affiliated with the Assemblies of God, USA, and accredited by the Association of Biblical Higher Education (ABHE). The college celebrated 70 years of operation during this study, while the graduate school was founded six years prior to the study. This project will focus on students in the undergraduate program, as these are the students with whom I spend much my time and are most fitting to the aim and scope of the study.

22. This distinction is made to establish the tradition of worship and education at TBCGS. Rick M Nañez, a Pentecostal scholar, sharply addresses an historical concern in Pentecostal theological thought: "Yet, too often many of us within the Pentecostal-Charismatic community fail in our conviction of and passing for [a thoughtful] approach to the life of faith. We tend to worship the act of worship itself, retaliate against detailed, doctrine-packed sermons, court a fondness for entertainment in the sanctuary, and exhibit marks of the addiction to the 'feel-goods.'" It is appropriate to emphasize here that TBCGS does not align with such "non-thinking" communities, but that of thoughtful Pentecostalism. Nañez. *Full Gospel, Fractured Minds?*, 36.

23. In this role, I teach undergraduate courses focusing on the church's ministry to emerging generations (children, youth and emerging adults), and pastoral ministry through care and counseling. Foundational throughout courses on the church's ministry to emerging generations is a holistic view, based off of much of the research included in this project. In addition to my faculty role, I also bring nearly 20 year of pastoral ministry experience spanning across all generations.

and a half,[24] causing a host of resources within the realm of religion to be aimed at the overall spiritual formation[25] and the church's ministry to this age group.[26]

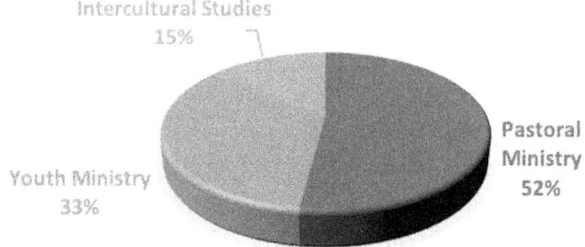

FIGURE 1: STUDY GROUP FIELD OF STUDY

Intercultural Studies 15%
Youth Ministry 33%
Pastoral Ministry 52%

Arnett, who coined the term "emerging adult," theorizes that this transitional phase cannot be summed up simply as either an extended adolescence or in the traditional idea of young adulthood. Emerging adults in twenty-first century America find themselves in a unique category.[27] A more precise examination of characteristics for this age group will be unpacked later in this project, but it is important to lay the groundwork early as to the context of this study through a cursory identification of traits identified in this age group. The common historical error in studying emerging adults has been to focus on what they are *becoming* while neglecting what they currently *are*.[28] As such, this study will be done with an eye focused on the

---

24. See especially Arnett. *Emerging Adulthood.*

25. See for example Christian Smith's work in both Smith, *Souls in Transition* and Smith, *Lost in Transition*; also Dunn, *Shaping the Journey of Emerging Adults*, and Setran and Kiesling, *Spiritual Formation in Emerging Adulthood.*

26. See for example the work of Fuller Youth Institute: Powell et al., *Growing Young*; also Kimball, *They Like Jesus But Not the Church.*

27. In Arnett's words, "This period is not simply an 'extended adolescence,' because it is very different from adolescence—much freer from parental control, much more a period of independent exploration. Nor is it really 'young adulthood,' since this term implies that an early stage of adulthood has been reached, whereas most young people in their twenties have not made the transitions historically associated with adult status—especially marriage and parenthood—and most of them feel they have not yet reached adulthood. It is a new and historically unprecedented stage of the life course, so it requires a new term and a new way of the thinking." Arnett, *Emerging Adulthood*, 2.

28. Arnett, *Emerging Adulthood*, 23.

research guiding the current understanding of emerging adulthood and the world in which they live and operate.

It is also important to establish a foundational understanding of the culture from which these young people emerge. In his foundational work on secularism, *A Secular Age*, Charles Taylor notes that Western culture has been moving in the direction of secularism for quite some time. In order to understand the cultural milieu of today's emerging adults, it is necessary to develop at least a cursory view of Taylor's characterization of the secular, alongside above noted contributions from scholars such as Berger and Schaeffer, in unpacking the dichotomization of public life in contemporary society.[29] As this secular viewpoint has become the predominant influence on Western worldview over the last several decades, emerging adults have been raised in a world that considers secularism the most objective viewpoint. Emerging adults as a whole, including college students, have been impacted by this shift. With this in mind, it is important to develop a foundational understanding of the secular worldview and how this has come to influence the place of faith in the lives of emerging adults.

This cultural phenomenon is imperative to consider in a study on emerging adulthood as one understands the identity-forming nature of this period.[30] Erik Erikson identified the third pillar of identity as a way of making sense of everything.[31] Taylor's claim regarding secularism presents an especially troubling prospect for emerging adulthood, as religion addresses questions regarding issues of "ultimate concern," as identified by theologian Paul Tillich.[32] These existential questions about what truly matters and what one's life means in light of mortality make it clear that the theological college must be aware of the effects of such a culture, and intentionally

---

29. Taylor's view of secularism will be fleshed out more fully in chapter two, but a central component of his theory is best understood through a contemporary question of the term religion: "If one identifies this with the great historic faiths, or even with explicit belief in supernatural beings, then it seems to have declined. But if you include a wide range of spiritual and semi-spiritual beliefs; or if you cast your net even wider and think of someone's religion as the shape of their ultimate concern, then indeed, one can make a case that religion is as present as ever." Taylor, *A Secular Age*, 427.

30. Arnett, *Emerging Adulthood*, 212.

31. Erickson, *Identity: Youth and Crisis*. Arnett notes that Erikson uses the term "ideology" throughout this explanation, but "he conceded that this term has pejorative connotations that he did not intend." The more widely accepted contemporary terminology, and still in line with Erikson's intention, is "Worldview." Arnett, *Emerging Adulthood*, note 1 on page 354.

32. Tillich, *Dynamics of Faith*.

work toward a reclamation of the language of faith. These questions of identity pose potentially the most daunting challenge set before American Christianity in the twenty first century.[33]

In this text, I seek to understand the impact of this cultural shift, especially during such a formative time as emerging adulthood, when a recognition of one's worldview is taking shape.[34] A formation of a worldview is when each person develops a mental or conceptual universe which provides the foundation by which one answers the fundamental questions of life: Who are we? Where did we come from? What is the purpose of life?[35] Al Wolters, Professor Emeritus of Religion a Redeemer University College, recognizes this as a sort of "mental map" that is necessary by nature for rational and reasonable beings.[36] Emerging adulthood is the key stage of development in which this sort of identity development takes place.[37]

A recognition of the secular viewpoint prevalent in twenty-first century culture, then, is foundational for a study on emerging adults as it forms the underlying worldview of the society in which this generation has grown to understand the world around them. It is also clear that this worldview influences students entering theological training and that this understanding central is imperative to the task of identifying the role of the colleges raising up young ministers.

In addition to understanding the underlying philosophical worldview in which emerging adults live, an examination of actual behavioral patterns is important to consider. As already noted, both Arnett's and Smith's studies on emerging adulthood have given definition to this formational period. It is no coincidence that the sociological findings of studies such as these

---

33. Dean makes this statement in light of Volf. *Exclusion and Embrace*. Volf is identified by Dean as the one who has made the most pointed application of this question for the contemporary American church.

34. Katariina Salmela-Aro, Kaisa Aunola, and Jari-Erik Nurmi note that "the third decade of life is a period during which individuals are faced with more transitions and life decisions than at any other stage of life. These include those related to the transition from education to work, starting a career, initiating an intimate relationship, and starting a family. It has also been found that people perceive these transitions and role changes as important markers of the transition to adulthood." Salmela-Aro et al., "Personal Goals During Emerging Adulthood."

35. Sire. *The Universe Next Door*.

36. Wolters, *Creation Regained*, 4.

37. For a brief history of the concept of worldview from a Christian perspective see Wolters, "On the Idea of Worldview and Its Relation to Philosophy," in *Stained Glass* ed. by Marshall et al., 65–80.

show signs of the worldview discussed above. In both studies a high level of pluralism in moral and religious beliefs were evident, clearly reflecting the tenets of secularism. For example, Smith notes that most emerging adults come out of a sort of "pick and choose" religion and a belief that religion's purpose is essentially to serve them and to give them what they need.[38] Arnett recognizes this in the limited appeal of religious services for most emerging adults, specifically because of the emphasis of collective rather than individual expressions of faith, which emerging adults seem to take as a compromise of their individuality.[39] Although others have recognized a marked pluralism in American religious culture, it is sensible to conclude that this pluralism—at least in the lives of emerging adults—is actually a religious individualism; a secular worldview that has relegated religion to a discussion of personal and subjective values.

This religious individualism will be important to monitor alongside what Taylor identifies as a "colossal" cultural shift toward immanentization, or the idea that one operates within and relies on oneself only. Taylor believes that many people see nothing wrong in living for purely immanent goals: "they live in a way that takes no account of the transcendent."[40] This leads to a sort of "shrinking" of God, in which God comes to be *about* man, therefore causing an immense shift in power to where the human—the individual—is at the center of all meaning.[41] Cornelius Plantinga Jr., former President of Calvin Theological Seminary, offers a summary of just such a possibility in what he calls an "ego-centered culture." He says this is where, "wants become needs (maybe even duties), the self replaces the soul, and human life denigrates into the clamor of competing autobiographies. In this culture, one becomes fascinated centrally with a subjective emphasis on one's feelings. In such a culture and in the throes of such fascination, the self exists to be explored, indulged and expressed but not disciplined or restrained."[42] Such a culture of immanent thinking promotes a shallow

---

38. Smith, *Soul Searching*, 157.
39. Arnett, *Emerging Adulthood*, 219.
40. Taylor, *A Secular Age*, 143.

41. James K.A. Smith identifies this immanence in the preface to his commentary on Taylor's work in this way: "Your neighbors inhabit what Charles Taylor calls as 'immanent frame'; they are no longer bothered by 'the God question' *as* a question because they are devotees of 'exclusive humanism'—a way of being-in-the-world that offers significance without transcendence. They don't feel like anything is missing." Smith, *How (Not) to be Secular*, viii.

42. Plantinga, *Not the Way It's Supposed to Be*, 83.

worldview that focuses on oneself almost exclusively, strikingly similar to that of the worldview identified in the NSYR.

It will be useful for us, then, to take a constructive approach toward emerging adulthood, even in light of the discouraging findings of the NSYR. The cultural fascination which identifies supposedly unique problems within emerging generations is frankly not helpful in identifying a better way forward and should be used primarily as a challenge to the theological campus culture in how to better interact with this generation and the culture in which they live and operate.[43]

An example of this can be found in the contrast between the NSYR and Arnett's conclusions surrounding emerging adulthood. In the NSYR, Smith identifies most emerging adults as religious and moral individualists, meaning that they identify such tenets as matters of individual choice and place a high value on tolerance for the individual choices of others. Smith sees this individualism specifically as a sign that emerging adults are "adrift"[44] and lines up this individualism with a sort of self-centered perspective on the world.[45] Arnett, however, takes issue with this characterization, noting other distinctions of emerging adulthood which demonstrate a strong connection to communal commitments and emphasizes the fact that much shared life for this age period—marriage, children, employment—remains a hypothetical future concept. Because of this, emerging adults tend to define their life goals in self-centered terms, but most recognize that these goals will change in time. Emerging adults find themselves in a naturally self-focused time of life, independent of parental oversight but not yet focused on new family ties.[46] Counter to Smith's "self-centered" understanding, then, Arnett sees the "self-focused" nature of emerging adulthood as a

---

43. It is notable that this theory finds support in a similar context. In Fuller Youth Institute's Churches Engaging Young People study, which included emerging adults, "empathizing with today's young people" was identified as one of the key strategies employed in churches that successfully engage emerging generations. Powell et al., *Growing Young*, 88–125.

44. Smith, *Lost in Transition*, 60.

45. As an interesting perspective on this view, Craig Detwiler offers a thought regarding popular magazines from Paul Stookey of the singing group Peter, Paul, and Mary: "They used to be called *Life* (about life), then it was *People* (not about life, but just about people), then it was *Us* (not even about all people, but just about us), then it was *Self* (not even about us). It's a question of how we extend ourselves into the world." Detwiler, *Selfies*, 12.

46. Arnett, *Emerging Adulthood*, 243.

natural and healthy condition. For this reason, we will approach emerging adults not as "self-centered" but as "self-focused" in nature.

Recent research would seem to suggest that Arnett's position is correct, identifying college students' seemingly blissful self-centered social media presence as a myth. In a study surveying a diverse cross section of American college students, Donna Freitas discovered a pervasive pressure surrounding social media in the lives of college students: "the importance of *appearing* happy."[47] Craig Detweiler says this generation has been "saddled with the burden of profile management"[48] while Freitas warns of the danger of such pressure: "In our attempts to appear happy, to distract ourselves from our deeper, sometimes darker thoughts, we experience the opposite effect. In trying to always appear happy, we rob ourselves of joy."[49] This statement does not paint the image of blissful self-centeredness. In fact, it portrays a self-image that is altogether insecure in one's identity. A reality that can be supported by studies on the contribution of American media,[50] as well as the introduction of such influence into other cultures[51]

For the reasons above it is important for us to take time—as we will do in a later chapter—to examine the impact of certain technological influences in the lives of emerging adults. For now, though, our concern is that the emphasis should be placed upon the issue of empathy with emerging adults in the twenty first century. To see the world through their eyes is to attempt to find a way forward for the Christian faith, while an overly critical eye might inadvertently accomplish the opposite.

It is important to recognize that self-focused emerging adults spend a good deal of time thinking about themselves as they navigate this period of emergence between youth and adulthood. This self-focus is not permanent, nor should it be seen in a negative connotation, but the goal is "to learn to

---

47. Freitas, *The Happiness Effect*, 38.
48. Detweiler, *Selfies*, 25.
49. Freitas, *Happiness Effect*, 38.
50. A study initiated by Brigham Young University lends an interesting perspective to this. This study found that 96 percent of girls and 87 percent of boys had encountered Disney princesses by the age of four. Girls who had engaged the most with this princess culture had the lowest body esteem. Lead researcher Sarah M. Coyne said, "Disney Princesses represent some of the first examples of exposure to the thin ideal . . . As women, we get it our whole lives and it really does start at the Disney Princess level, at age three and four." Coyne, "Pretty as a Princess."
51. Becker, "Television, Disordered Eating, and Young Women in Fiji."

stand alone as a self-sufficient person,"[52] as one who is prepared for the rigors of adulthood. It is partially due to this self-focused status that students' individual stories will be featured in the second part of this book. Emerging adulthood is a time of self-development one navigates before making commitments to family or vocation,[53] and as such, they operate in a self-focused mindset as they wrestle with questions of identity and worldview. A review of students' individual experiences will tap into their naturally self-focused mindset to uncover areas of development during their time on campus.[54]

Any serious student of theology, however, knows a self-focused approach to theology is inadequate at best and dangerous at worst.[55] It is for this reason that we will include an assessment of the impact of the campus—the classroom, interaction with faculty/staff, chapel services, and the "silent curriculum" including correspondence, media, and other non-spoken forms of campus communication, through group interviews with the selected study group.[56] As the studies noted above emphasize the individuality of religious belief, this study will attempt to examine how—or if—the theological campus has been able to gather students into the

---

52. Arnett, *Emerging Adulthood*, 14.

53. Arnett, *Emerging Adulthood*, 238.

54. This study has chosen to focus on students' ability to articulate stories of their own faith development and their use of these in ministry to others. This approach is intended to mirror studies which have focused on autobiographical memory, such as that discussed in Fioretti et al., "The Role of the Listener." In this review, the authors define these kind of personal narratives as "the stories people fashion to make meaning out of their lives."

55. Detweiler offers a helpful thought here: "When we take photos of ourselves, I urge us to consider Jesus's question, 'Who is it you are looking for?' Clarity of vision and keen auditory ability are a prerequisite for discipleship . . . We are often so enraptured with our screens that we fail to recognize the person next to us in class, on the bus, or across the border. I hope we will take time to notice what's going on with the person next to us. It could be a parent, a sibling, a roommate, a stranger. Hopefully, in studying our selfies, we start to see the beauty and wonder that reside within all of us. Technology is a wondrous gift loaded with possibilities and temptations. May the Spirit prompt us to think before we Snap or at least pray while we post, making it a godly discipline, a way to develop eyes to see." Detweiler, *Selfies*, 199–200.

56. Fioretti et al. note the importance of the makeup of the group in such a setting for sharing these stories: "Since narration is a co-construction of a story between listener and narrator, the listener's stance can influence emotion regulation processes of the storytelling. For example, a more agreeable listener was associated with emotion change, in terms of less negative emotions and more positive emotions after narration." Fioretti et al., "The Role of the Listener."

communal and historical Christianity, while maintaining their individuality in a developmental fashion throughout this key phase of identity formation.

2

Secularism and the Twenty-First-Century Emerging Adult

In order to understand the theological campus' role in raising up young leaders ready to proclaim the gospel, it is important first to unpack the background of the secular condition in which emerging adults have been raised and to examine its influence. Has secularism silenced the faith of the majority of American emerging adults? What are the implications if this is so? From where has this shift in the authority of faith language come? With a deeper understanding of these background issues, one can better understand the cultural milieu of the emerging adult and the role of a theological campus in preparing these students for ministry.

Contemporary Emerging Adulthood

First of all, it is important to present a limited understanding of emerging adulthood. As sociologists learn more about this emerging developmental category it is becoming clear that this is a key period of life in the shaping of one's identity, not least their faith identity. In a broad sampling of studies, across regions, ethnicities, and social classes, Americans consistently identify three criteria as definitive of adulthood:

1. Accept responsibility for yourself.
2. Make independent decisions.

3. Become financially independent.[1]

Several studies have recognized that this transition is taking place later than it has in previous generations. For example, the median age for one's first marriage is now five years later in both males and females than it was 50 years ago, as is the average age for a woman bearing her first child.[2] The deferred fulfillment of these common developmental milestones indicates that emerging adulthood has become a distinct developmental stage which must be considered. In this vein, young people in this transitional period must not be considered regarding what they are *becoming* but what they *are* right now.

This is especially important when one understands that emerging adulthood is now believed to span the ages of *at least* 18–25 years old, a period longer than infancy and early or middle childhood and nearly as long as the common view of adolescence. Emerging adulthood, and the developmental factors within this category, must be taken seriously if this group is to mature into healthy adults, much more so for those whom we are training as future ministry leaders.

Some scholars recognize this extended transitional period as indicative of cultural shifts and how these have impacted the road to adulthood.[3] Others point to a more diverse and complex culture, combined with

---

1. Arnett, *Emerging Adulthood*, 15.

2. Powell et al., *Growing Young*, 97. The median age for first marriage is now 26.5 for women and 28.7 for men, while the average age for women bearing their first child is 26.

3. This position is unpacked fully in Arnett, *Emerging Adulthood*, 2–7. Arnett recognizes Four Revolutions of the 1960s and 70s as the main contribution: The Technology Revolution, the Sexual Revolution, the Women's Movement, and the Youth Movement. In summary, Arnett argues that the Technology Revolution meant that more and more manufacturing jobs became automated, meaning that many young people were forced to continue their education beyond high school to specialize in an area in which they could enter an increasingly concentrated work force. The Sexual Revolution, particularly the invention of the birth control pill in 1964, opened the door to a new, "commitment-free" understanding of sexual intercourse. Young people for the first time were able to satisfy their sexual longings without concern of pregnancy, leading many to begin to delay marriage until later in their 20s. The Women's Movement meant that women had new prospects regarding both educational and career opportunities. Whereas women in earlier decades were under a heavy weight of pressure to find and marry early on, the Women's Movement opened new doors of opportunity where this was no longer the expectation, at least in the early 20s. The Youth Movement was just what it sounds like: a movement which glorified youth and denigrated adulthood. Whereas young people of earlier decades had been eager to "settle down" into adulthood, following generations saw this as the end of independence, spontaneity, and of endless possibilities.

extended levels of education required for today's challenging job market.[4] Either way, this extended transitional phase is best summarized as a generational identity crisis. Erik Erikson, the developmental psychologist behind much of the contemporary understanding of identity formation, recognized this phenomenon later in his career, already seeing in these years a sort of "prolonged adolescence"[5] where emerging adults ask identity-forming questions that were widely answered in previous generations during the adolescent period. The questions at the core of emerging adulthood are questions of meaning, of identity, belonging and purpose.[6] Inquiries such as these are at their core questions that a secular worldview is unprepared to answer and that much of Western culture effectively does not address.[7]

It is this reality that leads to the previously discussed self-focus of the emerging adult—living in a stage between childhood where one lives according to the standards of parents or other authority figures and adulthood where marriage, parental and employment responsibilities bring new commitments and obligations outside of oneself. Again, though, this should not to be seen in a negative light but rather as a natural in-between stage in which emerging adults are looking inward as they search for their identity. It is no coincidence that a notable instability[8] and a prolonged formation of one's identity coincide with one another.

Considering these characteristics alongside the secular worldview that is normative for today's emerging adults, it is not difficult to understand how the language of faith could be lost in this generation. To understand this better, one must examine what has happened from adolescence into emerging adulthood to see how this alteration has progressed over time.

4. Powell et al., *Growing Young*, 98.
5. Arnett, *Emerging Adulthood*, 9.
6. Powell et al., *Growing Young*, 95.
7. This is noted in the concept of professionalism in secular culture by Pearcey, *Total Truth*, 98: "In fact, the very concept of being 'professional' has come to have connotations of being secular. In the late nineteenth and early twentieth centuries, explains Christian Smith, there was a drive to professionalize all fields—which meant in practice throwing off a Christian worldview and cultivating a secular approach that was touted as *scientific* and *value-free*. The process was nothing less than a 'secular revolution,' Smith says."
8. Arnett, *Emerging Adulthood*, 11. This can be best understood in the context of an ever-changing Plan that changes as circumstances either require or allow. Arnett defines this "Plan" in this way: "Emerging adults know they are supposed to have a Plan with a capital 'P,' that is, some kind of idea about the route they will be taking from adolescence to adulthood."

Christian Smith's landmark research project, the National Study of Youth and Religion (NSYR), is a good sample for our consideration. Beginning in 2001 and continuing into the mid-2010s, Smith worked with a team of researchers to conduct the first stage of the NSYR, where over 3,000 teenagers and families were surveyed and interviewed trying to discover the heartbeat of faith for the American teenager. This study continued as Smith and his team conducted follow up interviews with these students into their late twenties.[9] Following the popular mindset of the day, Smith expected to find "contemporary teenagers [that were] deeply restless, alienated, rebellious, and determined to find something that is radically different from the faith in which they were raised."[10] What he found was quite different.

What the NSYR uncovered was an individualistic view of faith that holds a strictly instrumental view of religion, assuming that religion exists to help "individuals be and do what *they want*, and not as an external tradition or authority or divinity that makes compelling claims and demands on their lives, especially to change or grow in ways they may not immediately want to."[11] Put simply, the NSYR discovered that most American teenagers believed religion exists to make one feel good and to resolves one's problems; nothing more and nothing less.

Smith's findings are similar to Thomas E. Bergler's hypothesis in *The Juvenilization of American Christianity*,[12] which identifies this juvenilization as "the process by which the religious beliefs, practices, and developmental characteristics of adolescents become accepted as appropriate for all Christian ages."[13] In both the NSYR and Bergler's theory, the majority

---

9. The NSYR continued to follow their study group into emerging adulthood and these results are published in follow-up publications which will be used alongside the original NSYR findings in this paper: Smith, *Souls in Transition*; and Smith, *Lost in Transition*. These studies demonstrate a continual pattern related to much of what will be discussed in this paper from adolescence into emerging adulthood, but as much of the basic terms of the study were defined in the initial study results, the original NSYR will be noted throughout this paper. Any factors that waver from the initial NSYR in the subsequent studies on emerging adulthood will be discussed as such.

10. Christian Smith, *Soul Searching*, 119.

11. Smith, *Soul Searching*, 148.

12. Bergler, *The Juvenilization of American Christianity*. Although Bergler's examination is not specific to emerging adulthood, his premise remains applicable to this study. Bergler examines the impact of the "juvenilization" of Christian culture on the broader American church of the twenty-first century and how this has contributed to a shallow, consumeristic faith.

13. Bergler, *The Juvenilization of American Christianity*, 4.

of Christian emerging adults are mere consumers of religious goods and entertainment, with very little grasp of true faith, and even less ability to put words to their beliefs. This sort of consumerism is not new to American Christianity[14] and, in fact, is evident in the sort of religious pluralism evident throughout American history;[15] however, contemporary studies such as these presented by Smith and Bergler present a more pervasive consumerism in the mind of the twenty-first-century emerging adult.

A Secular Influence

One can certainly make the connection between this material worldview and the secular philosophy identified by Taylor,[16] especially the emphasis

---

14. Nathan O. Hatch's insightful survey of the democratic effect on American faith (Hatch, *The Democratization of American Christianity.*) which serves as an examination of the origins of church consumerism and its further development in contemporary American religious culture.

15. A helpful overview of some of the key people and events that have led these movements can be found in Stein. *Communities of Dissent.*

16. This philosophy is thoroughly addressed in Taylor, *A Secular Age*. Taylor identifies three forms of the term "secular." The first defines it as something referring to the earthly activities not considered sacred. Specifically, Taylor notes such practices as those within "common institutions and practices" namely the state, saying, "in our 'secular' societies, you can fully engage in politics without ever encountering God." This definition of secularism reflects classical or medieval accounts in which the secular might be equated to something like the temporal realm of politics or mundane vocations. All the world was religious—or at least a spiritual concept of the world was commonplace—during the medieval period, but the secular was recognized as that which fell outside of the sacred activities of man. This is the basis for Taylor's first form of "secular."

Secondly, Taylor sees the secular in terms of public spaces being subsequently emptied of any reference of God or reference to ultimate reality. These areligious spaces allegedly hold to no religious creed or belief, which those who support this theory see as an ultimate neutrality that religious belief cannot offer. Think again of Berger's public versus private sphere. Smith, *How (Not) to be Secular,* 21, says of this, "'According to secularization theory, as culture experiences modernization and technological advancement, the (divisive) forces of religious belief and participation wither in the face of modernity's disenchantment of the world. According to secularism, political spaces (and the constitutions that create them) should carve out a realm purified of the contingency, particularity, and irrationality of religious belief and instead be governed by universal, neutral rationality."

Schaeffer was certainly ahead of his time and Berger does well in recognizing that this mentality has spilled out onto the individual in the twenty first century. Both public space and individual now not only distinguish between secular and sacred tasks but take it a step further to claiming no religious belief or practice whatsoever. This is the basis for Taylor's second form of "secular."

on the temporal in secularism as "many people are happy living for goals which are purely immanent; they live in a way that takes no account of the transcendent."[17] This "titanic shift" has taken Western civilization from a society in which it was virtually impossible not to believe in God, to one in which faith is one possibility among others.[18] As emerging adults are products of this secular age,[19] they have given in to a new ideology which Taylor identifies as the disenchantment of the age.[20] From the premodern world in which power outside of oneself was assumed, to the secular age where all power is found *in* oneself. Andrew Root, Carrie Olson Baalson Professor of Youth and Family Ministry at Luther Seminary, recognizes this in that most young people no longer feel a need for God, and no sense of "gaping loss or sense of subtraction" when He is not present.[21] God has become largely irrelevant in the life of the average emerging adult.

Finally, Taylor addresses the crux of his foundational work on the topic: "A society is [secular] insofar as religious belief or belief in God is understood to be an option among others, and thus contestable (and contested)." This is especially important for this study because this is the worldview under which American emerging adults today have been raised. This understanding of secularism certainly aligns with the individuality of religious belief uncovered in both Arnett's and Christian Smith's studies on emerging adults, both of which will be addressed further below. This third form of "secular" gives philosophical understanding to the worldview of emerging adults in twenty-first century America, and thus is an important foundational understanding for this study. This form of "secular" is the central theme of this section and what should be understood throughout this paper when secularism is addressed.

17. Taylor, *A Secular Age*, 143.

18. Taylor, *A Secular Age*, 3.

19. Recently, secularism in America has been taken to task. Although many scholars note the marked decline of churches in many western cultures as the norm rather than the exception, they also note a turn in secularist theories. Berger, one of the foremost voices in this field of study, explains: "The assumption that we live in a secularized world is false. The world today . . . is as furiously religious as it ever was, and in some places more so than ever. This means that a whole body of literature by historians and social scientists . . . is essentially mistaken." Berger's conclusion addresses the fact that postmodernism has revealed a renewed sense of a belief in something beyond one's self. However, Taylor's definition of secular3, as outlined above, is not affected by this cultural shift toward postmodernism. In fact, it appears that this shift only strengthens Taylor's theory. Houtman and Aupers, "The Spiritual Turn and the Decline of Tradition."

20. Andrew Root notes that Charles Taylor referred to this as "the great unlearning of the languages of transcendence" at a public lecture at Duke University in 2014. Root, *Faith Formation in a Secular Age*, xii.

21. Root, "Faith Formation in a Secular Age."

Emerging Voices

Given this reality, it is no surprise that subjects of the NSYR displayed a self-centered idea of theology. Out of the study, Smith codified a sort of religious creed of its subjects:

1. A God exists who created and orders the world and watches over human life on earth.
2. God wants people to be good, nice, and fair to each other, as taught in the Bible and by most world religions.
3. The central goal of life is to be happy and to feel good about oneself.
4. God does not need to be particularly involved in one's life except when God is needed to resolve a problem.
5. Good people go to heaven when they die.[22]

Smith coined the term Moralistic Therapeutic Deism to define this theological worldview; moralistic in that the role of religion is to teach right behavior, therapeutic in that the central goal of God is to make one happy, and deistic in that it sees God as mostly uninvolved unless he is needed to make one's life better. The effects of such a shallow worldview are evident to recognize. Smith notes a particularly dangerous component at work:

> Therapeutic individualism defines the individual self as the source and standard of authentic moral knowledge and authority, and individual self-fulfillment as the preoccupying purpose of life. Subjective, personal experience is the touchstone of all that is authentic, right, and true. By contrast this ethos views the 'external' traditions, obligations, and institutions of society as inauthentic and often illegitimate constraints on morality and behavior from which individuals must be emancipated.[23]

Taylor's secular world is in view here, as well, as devotees of Moralistic Therapeutic Deism see any challenge to one's own comfort as something that must be eliminated. As mankind finds itself at the center, it once again finds that it has not simply removed God from the equation but has replaced Him. Moralistic Therapeutic Deism finds a fitting home within Taylor's secularism.

As mentioned above, Smith's follow-up study with emerging adults confirmed much of what was discovered in the original NSYR, and the presence of Moralistic Therapeutic Deism as a central religious creed is

---

22. Smith, *Soul Searching*, 162.
23. Smith, *Soul Searching*, 173.

no exception to this rule. Moralistic Therapeutic Deism remained very much "alive and well" in emerging adults, although the language associated with this worldview had been diluted by apparent life circumstances that had proven some of this idealism as unrealistic.[24] Even so, Smith concluded that "Moralistic Therapeutic Deism continues to be the faith of very many emerging adults. Often what emerging adults said in interviews . . . expressed a Moralistic Therapeutic Deism very close to the one they had articulated five years earlier."[25] The primary difference was that many emerging adults in the follow up study were drawn more to the practical themes of stability, structure, support, and guidance than to the teachings of faith.[26] Even in this, the follow up to the NSYR provides an example of an instrumental understanding of religion, with the exception that the ends had changed with time.[27]

Of specific concern here is how those interviewed in the NSYR struggled to verbalize their own views on faith. As mentioned previously, youth in the NSYR were found to be "incredibly inarticulate"[28] regarding their faith, so much so that the interviewers proposed that this might have been the first time these young people were asked such questions.[29] Not surprisingly, as Smith interviewed these young people five or six years later, this trend continued as they displayed an overwhelming religious disengagement. Several emerging adults defended this stance in saying that they had been raised with the understanding that one was never to speak of religion or politics, citing the danger of such contentious issues.[30] Note the tone of this statement: religion or politics—non-scientific matters—are "contentious" topics

---

24. Smith, *Souls in Transition*, 155.

25. Smith, *Souls in Transition*, 155.

26. Smith, *Souls in Transition*, 84–85.

27. Both Smith's study and other sources recognize the characteristics of MTD as more than self-inflicted ideology, however. Robert E. Webber notes: "The twenty-somethings appear to be the first generation of people coming out on the other side of a cultural paradigm shift. Wendy Murray Zoba writes, 'Generation X grew up *enmeshed* in their parents' revolutions, while the millennials are growing up *reacting* to the revolution.' According to William Strauss, 'The millennial generation is coming of cognition age at a time when the adult community has determined the conditions of childhood to be unacceptable.' He reports that boomers have become what *The New York Times* has dubbed a 'do as I say, not as I did' generation of parents." Webber, *The Younger Evangelicals*, 46.

28. Smith, *Soul Searching*, 131.

29. Smith, *Soul Searching*, 133.

30. Smith, *Lost in Transition*, 204.

to be avoided. They are not to be imposed on others but are private matters that should be kept to oneself as personal areas of conviction.

One can sense the challenge here of maintaining a Christian language in light of a culture that demonstrates no respect for the objective application of religious belief. Certainly, emerging adults are able to believe what they want to believe, but the secular culture in which they live relegates this to a private conversation that has no bearing on anything beyond personal taste. In this way, emerging adults are met with the challenge once described by British theologian Lesslie Newbigin: "We have been trained to use a language which claims to make sense of the world without the hypothesis of God . . . but then, for an hour or two a week, we use the other language, the language of the Bible."[31] Certainly for the emerging adult, this dualism has led to a loss of credibility for the language of faith. If society does not recognize the objective value of faith language, then it stands very little chance of making its way into the common vernacular of the standard emerging adult. But where does this dualism come from? That is the next question that must be addressed.

Berger recognizes that this shift first took place in the sphere of societal bounds, as religion was removed from "logical" conversation in culture to where it was relegated to the private sphere alone. Berger describes a "novel dichotomization of social life" that divides culture into the two categories of the public and private spheres. These spheres can be best understood in the language of "facts," meaning that they are binding on everyone, versus "values," which are subjective individual choice.[32] Scientific knowledge, recognized to be objective in its ability to be empirically proven, dominates the "facts" category, while religious faith finds itself relegated to the "values" side of the equation. This is where Newbigin's bilingual concern comes from and why Berger recognizes the individual as now "left to his own devices in a wide range of activities that are crucial to the formation of a meaningful identity, from expressing his religious preference to settling on a sexual lifestyle."[33] Once religion found itself in the subjective values category it no longer was afforded any right to speak objectively in the factual realm. Religion was no longer in the truth game.

Schaeffer was ahead of his time in his similar recognition of a divided concept of truth. He illustrates this with the image of a two-story building:

---

31. As quoted in Pearcey, *Total Truth*, 67.
32. Pearcey, *Total Truth*, 20.
33. Berger, *Facing Up to Modernity*, 133.

"In the lower story are science and reason, which are considered public truth, binding on everyone. Over against it is an upper story of noncognitive experience, which is the locus of personal meaning."[34] Once again, Schaeffer's conclusion recognized the growing view of science as objective truth, while religion was demoted to the subjective realm.

In this sense, science has risen since the Enlightenment through a "triumph of reason over ignorance and darkness" by cleansing the irrational elements from society in order to find the supposed true philosophy that can objectively address universal problems.[35] Of course, the idea of the empirical trumping all other forms of knowing might have been birthed in Enlightenment thought but years later it found a perfect dance partner in the modern era.

This is not only true of religion, but across the board in the humanities as schools take a postmodern approach, acting as though basics such as correct spelling and grammar are "forms of oppression imposed by those in power," while just down the hall objective truth still reigns supreme in the sciences.[36] Peter Kreeft, professor of philosophy at Boston College, sees in this educational dichotomy a perfect willingness "to believe in objective truth in science, or even in history sometimes, *but certainly not in ethics or morality.*"[37] It is no wonder that young people do not know how to speak of their faith, for they have simply never been taught the importance of such a practice.

Understanding the origins of this dualism makes it easier to understand where Taylor's philosophical proposition originates, his premise much more fathomable, that belief in God is now simply one option among many.[38] *A Secular Age* has already been addressed, however it is important to unpack Taylor's view further, realizing that this represents the larger cultural mosaic from which today's emerging adults have come. Emerging adults in the twenty-first century are a product of a culture that, in their memory, has always had a secular slant—an age in which the default has changed from a condition of belief, to a condition in which unbelief seems at first blush the only plausible outcome.[39] Taylor's work recognizes this

---

34. Pearcey, *Total Truth*, 21.
35. Lyon, "Secularization and Sociology."
36. Pearce *Total Truth*, 107.
37. As quoted in Pearce *Total Truth*, 107, emphasis original.
38. Taylor, *A Secular Age*, 3.
39. Taylor, *A Secular Age*, 12.

reality and foreshadows a result that looks much like the studies of Smith and Arnett on the religious lives of emerging adults.

Taylor also recognizes a theme apparent in Berger, Schaeffer, and Newbigin: that this seminal shift is not simply a matter of subtraction, or of removing a belief in God, but it is a matter of replacement. Although Taylor comes to this conclusion from a philosophical slant as compared to the sociological emphasis above, it is telling to see the similarity in conclusions. James K.A. Smith, Professor of Philosophy at Calvin University, summarizes Taylor's view saying, "it's not that our secular age is an age of *dis*belief; it's an age of believing otherwise."[40] Certainly one can hear the public and private spheres ringing through in Smith's conclusion.

It is important to keep this recognition in front of the academy that is tasked with training up pastors, youth pastors, children's pastors, evangelists, and so on—that the faith condition of American culture today is not a condition of the *loss* of God and of religious values, but it is the *replacement* of these. Taylor says it this way: "Modernity is defined not just by our 'losing' an earlier world, but by the kind of human culture we have constructed."[41] Any institution attempting to train ministers to proclaim the gospel must understand the culture in which they preach. Emerging adults in twenty-first century America need not only to understand the cultural condition surrounding them, but also how this culture has impacted them.

This shift in society has led to a shift in consciousness within the modern mindset in that fewer and fewer people see the objective value of religious faith and thus remove it from their awareness altogether.[42] In essence, if faith has no value publicly it loses its value privately. Or perhaps it is better understood that this value becomes less objective—even in one's own private life—and becomes more subjective. In this manner, the ultimate loss of faith is not the loss of church and/or moral adherence but is "the loss of the plausibility of transcendence, and the presumption that our world is only a natural and material place."[43] Emerging adults today are the victim of this cultural worldview. They are, as Smith sees it, narrative animals: "we define who we are, and what we ought to do, on the basis of what story we see ourselves in."[44] Emerging adults today largely live based

---

40. Smith, *How (Not) to be Secular*, 47.
41. Root, "Faith Formation in a Secular Age."
42. Berger, *The Sacred Canopy*, 113.
43. Root, "Faith Formation in a Secular Age."
44. Smith, *How (Not) to be Secular*, 25.

on the narrative of the secular society which they inhabit, even those who find themselves attending a Christian college or university. Those who are preparing for ministry must address this dichotomy and learn to walk in their faith identity beyond cultural bounds.

In short, for tomorrow's church leaders, this mentality must be overcome. The role of the theological campus in training young ministers is primarily a role of cross-cultural coaches; faculty and staff that are committed to helping students recover their lost identity. As emerging adults—even those with sights on a future in ministry—find themselves enveloped in this secular culture, they find themselves at a loss for words. They have been challenged their entire life as to whether their faith experience is relevant to the wider world, and it is the responsibility of theological education to renew this purpose and to re-teach the language of faith that this world is dying to hear.

It seems apparent that the above research proves that the secular condition of America has effectively silenced the faith of the majority of emerging adults. The implications as a whole are clearly concerning for American Christianity, but specifically for those entering vocational ministry. With this understanding, it is crucial that theological colleges take seriously their role in the identity formation of their students. The ministerial training of today's young people can no longer be seen primarily as an exchange of information but must be recognized as a formational activity. As it is clear to see from the above discussion, this is not simply a matter of re-teaching vocabulary or a particular set of theological terms but is a matter of reclaiming the *voice* of Christianity. Recovering the language of the faith is not a mere linguistic practice but is a form of re-building the culture and worldview of Christianity.

3

A Collegial Response

RECOGNIZING THE CHALLENGES OF twenty-first-century culture and its effect on emerging adulthood, it is important to assess the role of the theological campus in the reclamation of the Christian language, especially in preparing students for ministry. Why should this be a priority on the theological campus? What role does theological higher education play in preparing students to proclaim their faith in the world of the twenty first century?

Measuring the Influence of the Theological Campus

It is first of all important to recognize the influence of one's college experience. Higher education's roots are soaked in theological reflection, at least until the Enlightenment and modernism led to a definitive gap in this relationship. More recently there has been a renewal in this relationship, however, as public colleges and universities have gradually initiated institutional approaches to spiritual formation.[1] UCLA's study on spirituality in higher education highlighted this concern at the turn of the twenty-first century, saying that just as higher educational institutions were founded on spiritual, as well as intellectual growth, today's college student expects this sort of formational culture on their campus.[2] Although many college campuses have shifted their thinking toward a primarily intellectual

---

1. Reed, "Historical and Contemporary Approaches to Spiritual Formation in the University," 45.

2. Lindholm, "Spirituality in the Academy," 10–17.

environment, students continue to recognize something deeper at play in this formational period of their lives. Students recognize that college is a time not only for vocational development but also an opportune moment in the quest for wisdom. Parker J. Palmer, the distinguished Quaker scholar, says, "The task for higher education is to reclaim the wholeness of what we know about human knowledge: it is not just about distancing, it is about intimacy as well."[3] The wisdom that higher education was intended to pass along cannot be found through the exchange of information alone, but it was always intended to aim one's thoughts to higher planes of ultimate meaning and identity. It appears that students still desire this to be so.

A study of the Christian College Coalition (now the Coalition of Christian Colleges and Universities) in 1994 gives credence to this desire. This study found that respondents who were rooted in spiritual formation programs displayed characteristics of growing and mature Christians and noted that this was at least partially due to an ongoing conversation regarding their story throughout the life of the campus.[4] Likewise, this study cannot be limited to one aspect of the campus community (i.e., classroom discussion, chapel ministry, peer interaction) but must take into consideration the entirety of the college experience.

An Integrative Approach to Biblical Education

The theological campus is a unique environment in which to work through one's formation, most notably the Christian worldview within which Christian colleges operate. The theological campus is unique as a community in that it envelopes one's life in ways that other Christian communities do not.[5] Duane Liftin, former president of Wheaton College, distinguishes such an institution as "[seeking] to make Christian thinking systemic throughout the institution, root, branch, and leaf."[6] This is only accentuated as the theological campus seeks to train up vocational ministers. Certainly, the goal is not only to raise up leaders with a common knowledge but that the thinking instilled into students would lead to a shared faith identity. In this way, theological colleges are not only teaching a vocabulary

---

3. Palmer, "Toward A Spirituality of Higher Education," 80.
4. Reese, "Conversation Creates Culture," 158.
5. Reed, "The Power of Context," 95.
6. Reed, "The Power of Context," 96.

that informs their thinking but are infusing a language into students that becomes a key ingredient in their identity formation.

While we seek to understand the holistic impact of the theological college, it is assumed that the integration between one's story and God's story specifically takes place in the academic foci of the campus. This belief is supported by research that notes the importance of college faculty in the spiritual formation of students. Todd Hall, Professor of Psychology at Biola University, led a study entitled "Furnishing the Soul" which surveyed nearly two thousand Christian college students. This study found that faculty were cited in four out of the top ten "spiritually transformational influences" of college life.[7] The influence of faculty rated higher than chapel, community service and/or outreach programs, student leadership opportunities, or any other ministry programming. Theologian Paul Hoon said, "spiritual formation is by definition community formation . . . community is the matrix of growth . . . and the vertebrae of the community are the faculty."[8] As students navigate this transitional period of life, they look to faculty as guides in their story.

I recall a moment in my first year on faculty where the Vice President of Academics shared in a meeting that the faculty's job was to shape the conversation of the campus. With this in mind, professorship must be recognized as a higher calling than a purveyor of information. Faculty on a theological campus must recognize their role in this manner and that, as Palmer says, "In the very act of educating we are in the process of forming or deforming the human soul."[9] Especially in light of the culture in which emerging adults live and especially with the knowledge that these students will shape the church of tomorrow, faculty must be aware that their influence carries beyond the classroom and into the conversation of campus community. In essence, the role of the faculty is to re-form what culture might have deformed and help students to recapture their faith identity so that they are better prepared to proclaim it.

---

7. Balzer, "Leaving A Mark," 64.

8. Balzer, "Leaving A Mark," 63–64.

9. Palmer, "Toward A Spirituality of Higher Education," 75. James K.A. Smith sees something similar in his examination of what it means to be formed in Christian worship: "Now here's the crucial insight for Christian formation and discipleship: not only is this learning-by-practice the way our hearts are correctly calibrated, but it is also the way our loves and longings are *mis*directed and *mis*calibrated—not because our intellect has been hijacked by bad ideas but because our desires have been captivated by rival visions of flourishing." Smith, *You Are What You Love*, 21–22.

A Collegial Response

Arnett's research on emerging adults supports the importance of college faculty in this process, noting that one's childhood religious upbringing has much less to do with religious beliefs during emerging adulthood than in adolescence. In fact, Arnett's research indicates no statistical connection between one's childhood religious training and *"any aspect of their religious beliefs"* as emerging adults.[10] The main reason for this distinction in emerging adulthood: the gradual increase of influences on one's life outside of family. Arnett specifically notes the influence of college and how new influencers, such as one's college professors, often challenge previously held beliefs.[11] In many colleges and universities this represents the spiritual "deforming" that Palmer notes above; however, theological colleges must also understand this reality.

Specifically, the theological campus must recall valid criticism of Bible institutes that began to surface in the mid-twentieth century. These Bible institutes often narrowed their theological teachings to a spiritual inoculation to the world around them. This shallow teaching led to what religious historian Mark Noll refers to as "the intellectual disaster of fundamentalism."[12] Theological institutions must be better than this and identity not as a "bubbles" in which Christians come to be protected, but as intentional training grounds to better prepare to proclaim the message of the gospel. Faculty must equip its students both in preparation for vocational success, but also in learning the art of gospel proclamation for a world that is less familiar with the Christian faith perhaps than at any other time throughout American history.

This places an emphasis on faculty and others who influence students, not only in presenting accurate information, but also in the manner in which it is presented. As addressed above, this sort of formation cannot be attained through instruction alone, but it must be recognized that the role of faculty is much more that of an apprentice or a mentor than a classic instructor. Susan Reese, professor of spiritual formation at Sioux Falls Seminary, contends that conversations are the ideal tool for this outcome on the college campus. She says that emerging adults are not so much looking for answers as they are seeking people "who will allow their questions to be voiced and their story to be told."[13] In this environment students

10. Arnett, *Emerging Adulthood*, 224.
11. Arnett, *Emerging Adulthood*, 226.
12. Carpenter, "The Mission of Scholarship in the New Millennium," 7.
13. Reese, "Conversation Creates Culture," 160.

will experience an integration between their own experiences and their academic understanding. Any school that looks to foster the wisdom of Scripture must be doing so in a way that speaks to emerging adults in a relational manner that helps them to connect the dots where American secular culture has failed to do so.

This integration of learning outside of the classroom is only accentuated by a quick examination of the current generation of college student, as Millennials have made way for Gen Z to take over the college campus. In a collaborative webinar presenting their study on Gen Z, the Barna Group and Impact 360 Institute shared that their research had uncovered a blatant distrust for public ads, news and TV in this generation.[14] This inherent distrust of public personas is perhaps not difficult to understand in light of the world in which Gen Z has been raised, a world in which carefully crafted public images are understood by many to be enhanced at best and counterfeit at worst. Even these young people themselves recognized their own concession to this public façade, noting a severe pressure to appear happy and successful online even when it is not true.[15] This places a new pressure on college faculty to back up personally what is shared from the front of the classroom, and to employ a more conversational tone of apprenticeship with this generation of students.

The question that must be answered in reply to this information, then, is whether the preponderant models of Christian higher education are prepared to answer the current challenges. The prevailing approach in most contexts is that of an integration model. This model can be traced back to two main proponents in the mid-1970s, namely Arthur Holmes, former professor of philosophy at Wheaton, as well as Nicholas Wolterstorff, former professor of philosophy at Calvin College, the Free University and later at Yale. The integration model has its roots in an era of American higher education where Christian scholars were trying to reclaim their voice in the academy. As modernism had pushed theology to the side, more and more young Christian scholars saw the need to prove their intellectual mettle with graduate degrees from prestigious universities. Although they recognized the need for such academic credentials, these young evangelicals recognized that they would not agree with many of the claims of their

---

14. This study was originally published as *Gen Z: The Culture, Beliefs and Motivations Shaping the Next Generation*. Barna Group and Impact 360 Institute, 2018. The five-part webinar can be accessed at http://www.whoisgenz.com.

15. *Gen Z*, 19.

illustrious faculty. In fact, these students often assumed some of the key thinkers in their disciplines were gravely mistaken.[16]

The integration model acted as a positive response of scholars who recognized what Christian faith had to offer to scholarship. Although fundamentalist Christianity had for years sought to attack liberal arts institutions and to defend the faith from them, proponents of the integration model sought to emphasize the mutual positive contribution that faith and academia shared. Holmes argued that Christian scholarship offered an integrated worldview through the light of God's creative and redemptive nature as opposed to the fragmented view that dominated the academy.[17] Christian scholarship, then, was an attempt at bringing together one's faith and one's academic focus and recognizing the validity of the conversation between the two.

Wolterstorff agreed with Holmes but considered more directly the concrete practices of the academy, specifically the inevitability of argument and debate in the learning environment. He saw that Christian scholars faced the same need as other learners in that learning takes place in the midst of the ongoing struggle of theories versus theories. For this reason, Wolterstorff recognized the need to identify a process by which one could intelligently choose between theories. He asserted that three beliefs were inherently involved in this process: data beliefs ("minimally tested assertions about reality with which a theory has to be consistent if it is to be acceptable"), data-background beliefs ("the kinds of evidence one is willing to accept as either supporting or undermining one's data beliefs"), and control beliefs ("larger or deeper convictions about what might constitute 'an acceptable sort of theory' in the first place").[18] Wolterstorff's theory was important because it gave Christian scholarship a place in the academy, recognizing that scholars from all backgrounds had to make decisions regarding the worthiness of certain claims in their field.

Wolterstorff's theory is especially important to understand in training up emerging adults as church leaders in a culture that belittles faith. Pearcey notes that every system of thought begins with an ultimate principle and that Christianity is not alone in this thinking: "If it does not begin with God, it will begin with some dimension of creation—the material, the

---

16. Jacobsen and Jacobsen, *Scholarship & Christian Faith*, 17.
17. Jacobsen and Jacobsen, *Scholarship & Christian Faith*, 19.
18. Jacobsen and Jacobsen, *Scholarship & Christian Faith*, 21.

spiritual, the biological, the empirical, or whatever."[19] In this way, theological students ought to recognize that Christian scholarship—and thus, proclamation—is much the same as other belief systems in that one's worldview is shaped out of some manner of thinking that begins with an ultimate principle. Christians are not alone in seeing the world through a particular lens but were perhaps some of the earliest to recognize and admit this fact. A theological student preparing to proclaim the gospel to a world which has marginalized the importance of faith must recognize that supposed objective beliefs also find their home in some ultimate principle, or faith. In teaching this and reclaiming the voice of faith, the theological college emboldens future ministers of the gospel to speak in confidence and to abandon the fear that their voice has no place in this world.

Abraham Kuyper, the influential neo-Calvinist theologian, famously resisted this idea that religion was merely private and personal, affirming this in his speech at the dedication of the Free University by saying, "there is not one single inch of the created world over which Jesus Christ does not say, 'This too is mine.'"[20] Christian faculty, too, should proclaim this with the same boldness, recognizing that the integration model has opened the door to a balance of scrutiny which both strengthens and holds in check Christian scholarship.

Wolterstorff rightly saw the integration view as one that should provide Christian scholars with great confidence in proclaiming their faith,[21] however, this self-assurance does not come without difficulty. Robert Wuthnow, former chair of the Department of Sociology and Director of the Princeton University Center for the Study of Religion, claims that a Christian worldview combined with an integrated view of scholarship imposes an extra set of questions on the Christian scholar—"questions of meaning, value, responsibility, and sometimes questions of pain and loss."[22] These are not questions that are limited to the Christian scholar, nor are they distinctly religious, but religious scholars of all kinds find it harder to put aside these questions in their own quest for understanding. In a faith that claims to be rooted in questions such as these, it can be difficult for the Christian scholar to admit their lack of answers. However, this struggle is not new and should be embraced and passed along to those who will continue to

---

19. Pearcey, *Total Truth*, 41.
20. Evans, "The Calling of the Christian Scholar-Teacher," 29.
21. Jacobsen and Jacobsen, *Scholarship & Christian Faith*, 22.
22. Jacobsen and Jacobsen, *Scholarship & Christian Faith*, 46.

carry on the message of Christianity, for it is not answers that the Christian seeks, but the One who knows all.

In reality, these questions push against a vice Thomas Aquinas identified as pusillanimity, or smallness of soul. Aquinas recognized this as "a habit of shrinking back from all that God was calling you to be out of fear of failure, a sense of inadequacy, a feeling of powerlessness or incompetence."[23] The questions that Wuthnow identifies in the Christian scholar, then, also ought to find a home in the student who seeks to fulfill God's call even in light of their own inadequacy. These questions seek a higher meaning for which the theological college should not only be equipped to offer but that should be at the center of its educational mission.

Higher meaning, though, does not usually come without times of questioning, which presents a challenge to the integration model. The chief concern of this model—a tendency to "promote conflict rather than conversation" and to impose religious authority over a discipline instead of expanding the dialogue[24]—could be troublesome in the academic environment of the twenty-first century. Paul J. Wadell, professor of theology and religious studies at St. Norbert College, demonstrates this danger, saying that "in a culture where there are no truths, only opinions, teachers and students are equals and differences are resolved not by reasoned arguments, but by subtle intimidations."[25] Emerging adults today expect to collaborate in their learning experience and look to be co-creators of value in their education. Faculty will be well-served to understand this and that this means that a student's involvement in the classroom is only the beginning of their education.

In order to promote this level of engagement a theological campus must embrace the struggle of questioning emerging adults. In fact, this kind of struggle lies at the heart of spiritual formation in emerging adults:

> A student's spiritual passion is expanded and his or her faith challenged by observing and struggling through various stages of the journey: suffering, moral development, intellectual development, vocational/career transitions, Christian worldview and responsibility, life crisis, challenges, and revelation.[26]

---

23. DeYoung, "Pedagogical Rhythms," 26.
24. Jacobsen and Jacobsen, *Scholarship & Christian Faith*, 46.
25. Wadell, "Teaching As A Ministry of Hope," 123.
26. Reese, "Conversation Creates Culture," 161.

Some describe these struggles or crises as "thresholds;" as times of transition when students are likely ready for change, are moving from one stage of spiritual formation to another, are experiencing worldview shifts and moving into a new stage of faith, ultimately marking the beginning of a new stage of being.[27] In recognizing the value of struggle in emerging adults, the theological campus is best served to keep in mind Wuthnow's words: "Christian scholarship is ultimately a matter of living the questions; it is never a matter of thought alone."[28] It ought to be expected, then, that Nemeck and Coombs' three thresholds—restlessness, transition, and stabilization[29]—would be evident in the stories of theological students. As students share their stories careful attention must be applied to identify these three thresholds; how the students have moved through these whilst on campus, what specific influences helped them along the way, and potentially how students have grown over time.[30]

Perhaps a good way to recognize this task is through Palmer's idea of a gospel epistemology,[31] which presents the gospel less as an ethic or a way of living and more in terms of a way of knowing. As the theological campus seeks to undo the spiritual deformation of the secular worldview which has accompanied emerging adults throughout their development, the gospel must become central in the understanding of what can be known. As Palmer says, "at its deepest reaches, the gospel is a way of knowing, and if we cannot recover that way of knowing, I do not really think we can do Christian higher education or form our students in a Christian ethic."[32] This gospel epistemology encompasses four distinct traits that will serve as counterbalances against a secular worldview and will build a strong Christian worldview which will help students recapture the language of faith.

27. Reese, "Conversation Creates Culture," 161.
28. Jacobsen and Jacobsen, *Scholarship & Christian Faith*, 60.
29. Reese, "Conversation Creates Culture," 161.
30. Particularly, students in my interviews had endured an exceptionally challenging previous semester in the spring of 2018, as two students were killed in two separate car accidents just three weeks apart. It was expected that these experiences would be addressed by at least some students, as the impact of these losses was felt deeply throughout the campus. However, none of the students directly referenced these deaths. This is not to say that these events were not an influence on these students, but that perhaps they were not as closely attached with these students and so these events did not hold the personal nature here as they did for others on campus.
31. This idea is more fully unpacked in Palmer, "Toward a Spirituality of Higher Education," 81–83.
32. Palmer, "Toward a Spirituality of Higher Education," 81–83.

A Collegial Response

First of all, this gospel epistemology teaches that truth is personal. Truth in matters of faith is not simply propositional and about getting facts straight. The Christian faith has fallen into this trap over the last century, believing that if it could just prove beyond a reasonable doubt the faith that it proposes that unbelievers would be forced to believe. However, the pluralism and individualism displayed in emerging adults today demonstrates that this approach is not working. In fact, even as much of Western culture has moved beyond a modern into a postmodern worldview which largely rejects the ultimate authority of the empirical, the church still finds itself fighting this same old battle.

Theological colleges, in preparing young men and women for ministry, must recognize the personal nature of truth. Christianity does not offer objectification or propositional truth, but instead offers truth in the person of Jesus. Palmer says, "Each of us are called to the personhood of truth, to be an incarnation of truth, and not just to recall propositions about truth."[33] As we mentioned before, one of the weaknesses of the integration model of Christian higher education is its confrontational manner. Certainly, a critical stance toward the secular worldview of the twenty-first century needs to be a component of theological higher education, but this is a reminder that the goal is not to win an argument but to embody the faith. In this way, staff and faculty should live by the mantra of Paul: "Be imitators of me, as I am of Christ" (1 Cor 11:1).

Secondly, the gospel epistemology recognizes truth as communal. In light of what has been discussed regarding the individualism of emerging adults, this is a particularly important matter that must be addressed. In an age that is pushing higher education to be more accessible, the communal aspect of education cannot be lost and must be promoted especially to those who seek to speak the gospel into this age.

Palmer makes the point that truth "is to be spoken and lived in community and tested in a continuing communal process of dissent and consent."[34] Many of the emerging models of ministry education—online, local church campuses, etc.—do not allow for such diverse interaction. Theological campuses need to emphasize their role in this manner and must practice this in reality. In order to raise up emerging leaders within a secular realm, gospel truth must be grasped in community, and that

---

33. Palmer, "Toward a Spirituality of Higher Education," 82.
34. Palmer, "Toward a Spirituality of Higher Education," 82.

community must allow for the natural struggle of students who are reforming their minds around a biblical worldview.

Thirdly, the gospel epistemology says that truth is mutual and reciprocal. While many institutes of higher education claim a dedication to the pursuit of truth, theological colleges recognize that truth not so much evades mankind as much as mankind evades truth. It is only through faith and spiritual maturity that one finds themselves in a place where they are ready to begin this pursuit.

Palmer says, "It would be a very interesting thing if academics could put down the instruments of pursuit long enough to allow truth to find us! That would lead to a very different way of teaching and learning, one we might call the gospel way."[35] This "gospel way" points to the need for a faculty that is in development themselves; professors who not only proclaim truth but that continue in their quest for deeper understanding. In this model, students become party to the process and are inspired to grow in their faith as they see in their mentors.

Lastly, the gospel epistemology says that truth is transformational. In the contemporary worldview truth lacks the power to transform because it is the object of the one who "controls meaning, who controls institutions, and who controls the earth."[36] Objectivism like this gives the illusion that mankind is in charge, but Christians know better. Christians know that truth is not something to be controlled but is something to discover and to live into in a way that invites one to change.

Palmer says that gospel truth is transformational truth and "says that we are not masters but are subject to powers larger than ourselves—and that we are blessed with the chance to be co-creators of something good if we are willing to work in harmony with those larger powers."[37] In training up Christian leaders, and especially those who will proclaim the gospel in the church of tomorrow, theological campuses must present truth as from God and as an invitation to a transformed life. Emerging adults live in a world that has promoted individualism and consumerism to the point that they are in danger of buying into a world that revolves around themselves. A theological college raising up young Christian leaders must be a reeducation of this way of thinking.

---

35. Palmer, "Toward a Spirituality of Higher Education," 83.
36. Palmer, "Toward a Spirituality of Higher Education," 83.
37. Palmer, "Toward a Spirituality of Higher Education," 83.

A Collegial Response

    Certainly, there is more that could be addressed regarding the role that the theological campus must take, but this discussion lays out a basic understanding of the importance of theological higher education in this process, as well as some ideas as to how it can address such a concern. In reforming what this secular age has deformed, the theological campus plays a key role in helping emerging adults reclaim the language of Christianity so that they are better prepared to proclaim their faith as they graduate into vocational ministry.

4

Screens Disciple

IN *FAITH FOR EXILES*, David Kinnaman and Mark Matlock attempt to present a better form of discipleship for contemporary emerging adults. In this project the authors make the simple yet profound statement, "Screens demand our attention. Screens *disciple*."[1] The constant presence of technology and its effect on emerging adults is impossible to deny. This deep connection between emerging adults and their screens is another factor that must be considered regarding their ability and willingness to proclaim their faith.

The pervasive nature of technology in the lives of emerging adults is demonstrated clearly in the research done by Kinnaman and Matlock, which notes that the average fifteen-to-twenty-three-year-old takes in almost 20 times as much screen media in the average week as they do spiritual content.[2] Tony Reinke, in his book *12 Ways Your Phone is Changing You*, further unpacks this reality, noting that the average American checks his or her smartphone approximately 81,500 times a year, or once every 4.3 minutes.[3] Some even estimate that the Facebook product line (Facebook, Messenger, and Instagram) now occupies at least fifty minutes

---

1. Kinnaman and Matlock, *Faith for Exiles*, 25
2. Kinnaman and Matlock, *Faith for Exiles*, 26.
3. Reinke, *12 Ways Your Phone is Changing You*, 43. Other sources have attempted to estimate these numbers. Notably Eadicicco, "Americans Check Their Phone 8 Billion Times a Day," which estimated that Americans check their phones at least forty-six times per day (seventy-four per day for 18–24-year-olds), and Andrew-Gee, "Your Smartphone Is Making You Stupid, Antisocial, and Unhealthy. So Why Can't You Put It Down?," which figures the number to be more like 150 times per day.

of the average American's day,[4] 25% more than the average American family spends together in quality time.[5] Scientific studies are even beginning to compare habitual Facebook use with addictive behavior such as drug abuse.[6]

Some of those who have played a role in developing the technology related to human connectivity are beginning to speak out and are admitting a consciousness to its risks. Sean Parker, formerly the president at Facebook, recently conceded that the social media platform "was designed to hook users with spurts of dopamine, a complicated neurotransmitter released when the brain expects a reward or accrues fresh knowledge."[7] He admitted that this technology was designed with a conscious understanding that it was exploiting a vulnerability in human psychology. Chamath Palihapitiya, former vice-president of user growth at Facebook, said to an audience at Stanford Business School, "I feel tremendous guilt. I think we all knew in the back of our minds . . . something bad could happen . . . The short-term, dopamine-driven feedback loops that we have created are destroying how society works. It is eroding the core foundations of how people behave."[8] This only becomes more troubling as research becomes available that links more screen time for young people to a higher likelihood of unhappiness.[9]

Tristan Harris, a former product manager at Google, has spent the past several years addressing these regrets through a non-profit called Time Well Spent. Harris says, "Smartphones are literally using the power of billion-dollar computers to figure out what to feed you. That's why you

---

4. Stewart, "Facebook Has 50 Minutes of Your Time Each Day. It Wants More," cited in Reinke, *12 Ways Your Phone is Changing You.*

5. Renner, "American Families Spend Just 37 Minutes of Quality Time Together Per Day, Survey Finds."

6. Molloy, "Facebook addiction 'activates same part of the brain as cocaine.'"

7. Andrew-Gee, "Your Smartphone Is Making You Stupid."

8. Andrew-Gee, "Your Smartphone Is Making You Stupid."

9. Twenge, *iGen*, 77. Although Twenge is reluctant to attach causality to this conclusion, she hints at recent research pointing to this fact: "These analyses can't unequivocally prove that screen time causes unhappiness; it's also possible that unhappy teens spend more time online. However, three recent studies suggest that screen time (particularly social media use) does indeed cause unhappiness. One study asked college students with Facebook pages to complete short surveys on their phones over the course of two weeks—they'd get a text message with a link five times a day and report on their mood and how much they'd used Facebook. The more they'd used Facebook, the unhappier they later felt. However, feeling unhappy did not lead to more Facebook use. Facebook use caused unhappiness, but unhappiness did not cause Facebook use." Twenge, *iGen*, 78.

can't look away . . . [someday] we're going to look back and say, 'Why on earth did we do this?'"[10] The influence of technology is undeniable; the effects are only beginning to become clear.[11] As journalist Clive Thompson aptly put it, "The one thing that both apocalyptics and utopians understand and agree upon is that every new technology pushes us toward new forms of behavior while nudging us away from older ones."[12] In other words, screens *disciple*.

The Relationship Between Technology and Proclamation

For a work such as this it is important to maintain an intentional focus. This chapter is not meant to serve as a comprehensive examination of theological views on technology.[13] It is, however, aimed at demonstrating the effects of technology on emerging adults' ability to proclaim their faith as well as to assist those who seek to disciple this generation in better understanding

---

10. Andrew-Gee, "Your Smartphone Is Making You Stupid."

11. The power of screens is evident in the developed world, but perhaps a clearer demonstration can be gathered by noting the effect on fresh eyes. Anne Becker's research in rural communities in Fiji provides this perspective. Within three years of Western television's arrival, young women throughout these remote villages developed a preoccupation with the shape of their body and began engaging in purging behavior in an attempt to control their weight. Young women who seemingly demonstrated feelings of sufficiency prior to the arrival of Western technology were now haunted by feelings of inadequacy. Indeed, screens disciple. Becker, "Television, Disordered Eating, and Young Women in Fiji: Negotiating Body Image and Identity during Rapid Social Change" cited in Detweiler, *Selfies*, 32.

12. Thompson, *Smarter Than You Think*, 8.

13. Others have attempted to tackle a theological construct for one's use of technology. Craig M. Gay theorizes that advancement in technology might be a natural part of being human, but that the more recent shift form "tools" and "contrivances" that once *made use of nature* to "machines" which now seek to *overcome the limits of nature* demonstrate a sort of disconnect from an understanding and respect of God's creation. Gay, *Modern Technology and the Human Future*, 28.

Craig Detweiler sees something even more personal in one's relationship with technology: the search for the *imago dei* in the screen before us. He quotes Jill Walker-Rettberg saying, "perhaps the reason we feel the need to take another, and yet another selfie, is in part that we, as the surrealists wrote in 1928, never seem able to create a photo that will 'fully correspond to what you want to see in yourself." Walker-Rettberg, *Seeing Ourselves Through Technology*: cited in Detweiler, *Selfies*, 119. Detweiler sees in one's screen the opportunity to look beyond the idealized image of oneself, and to recover the art of *contemplatio*, learning to see ourselves, our neighbors, and even God more clearly. Detweiler, *Selfies*, 192.

one of its unique challenges. How are digital natives impacted in their ability to proclaim the gospel in a world where communication has largely moved online? Technology's intuitive influence on this generation must be considered in understanding any shift in thinking or practice.

Does Technology Impact Witness?

First of all, it is important to determine whether technology has had a prominent influence on emerging adults in their proclamation of the gospel; namely, social media such as Facebook, Twitter, Instagram, Snapchat and so on, as these applications have most directly influenced the way emerging adults communicate.

Sherry Turkle, Abby Rockefeller Mauzé Professor of the Social Studies of Science and Technology at the Massachusetts Institute of Technology, notes the deep impact of digital communication on conversation in her book *Reclaiming Conversation*. She says, "Conversation implies something kinetic. It is derived from words that mean 'to tend to each other, to lean toward each other,' words about the *activity of relationship*, one's 'manner of conducting oneself in the world or in society; behavior, mode or course of life.'"[14] Conversing is less about taking turns in making statements and more about seeking connection; "you have to listen to someone else, to read their body, their voice, their tone, and their silences. You bring your concern and experiences to bear, and you expect the same from others,"[15] she says. In short, this kind of connection takes time and attention, something that is often lacking in the technological atmosphere of the twenty-first century.[16]

Technology has not only changed conversation in general, it has impacted faith proclamation directly. Kinnaman and Matlock note that in a recent study on this topic, six out of ten emerging adults said, "technology and digital interactions make me more careful about how and when I share my faith" (58 percent) and that "people are more likely now than in the past to see me as offensive if I share my faith" (61 percent). Two out of three said that people in today's culture are so busy with their screens that

---

14. Turkle, *Reclaiming Conversation*, 44.

15. Turkle, *Reclaiming Conversation*, 45.

16. Turkle describes a common reality of distraction as, "the typical American family is managing six or seven simultaneous streams of information . . . laptops, phones, a desktop, and of course, in the background, a television, perhaps two." Turkle, *Reclaiming Conversation*, 42.

they "are more likely to avoid real spiritual conversations" (64 percent).[17] It seems that technology has introduced novel challenges in relation to faith proclamation.

To dig deeper into this statement, it is helpful to examine emerging adults' experience with technology, specifically social media and its effect on the internal and external world of today's college student. Recognizing these effects help to identify the impact this shift in communication has had on faith proclamation and how the theological campus can better equip emerging adults for the technological world in which they live.

Internal Effects of Technology

The effect of technology on faith proclamation is made clearer when one first understands the internal importance of this medium in the life of the average emerging adult. Chap Clark led a lengthy immersive study into contemporary high school culture while he served as Chair of Christian Discipleship department and Professor of Practical Theology and Youth, Family, and Culture at Fuller Theological Seminary. From this study, Clark describes a troubling reality for adolescents which will be helpful in understanding a similar reality in emerging adults:

> By the time children, even the successful ones, reach high school and middle adolescence, they are aware of the fact that for most of their lives they have been pushed, prodded, and molded to become a person whose value rests in his or her ability to serve someone else's agenda. Whether they experience it from a coach, a schoolteacher, a parent, a music teacher, or a Sunday school counselor, midadolescents intuitively believe that nearly every adult they have encountered has been subtly out to get something from them.[18]

It is from this belief that Clark draws the conclusion that adolescents today have formed a sort of subculture that he identifies as "the world beneath."[19] It is notable that this kind of generational division is not completely new in adolescence—the origin of the contemporary concept of adolescence is based on a response to youth subculture identified in the early

---

17. Kinnaman and Matlock, *Faith for Exiles*, 25–27.
18. Clark, *Hurt 2.0*, 40–41.
19. A full explanation of this theory can be found in Clark, *Hurt 2.0*, 43–56.

twentieth century as the "youth problem"[20]—but Clark sees three issues that set this communal identity apart from previous generations of adolescence:

1. Adolescents believe they have no choice but to create this world, due to the lack of support from adult culture;
2. Adolescents are emotionally and relationally starved into this response;
3. Adolescents demonstrate a strong ability to create community in order to satisfy these deficiencies.[21]

Again, this theory is useful in understanding emerging adults in a similar context, not only because of their developmental proximity, but also recognizing similarity between their experiences. Consider the above descriptors of "the world beneath" in comparison to the conclusions of a study of college students by Donna Freitas, a research associate with Notre Dame's Center for the Study of Religion and Society:

> A "work hard, play hard" mentality often prevails on campus. Extremely stressed, high-achieving, incredibly busy college students work extraordinarily hard at their studies, sports, and activities during the week but then party like crazy and drink as heavily as they can on the weekend, *believing they "deserve" to engage in such behavior because they are so overburdened the rest of the time.* This mentality seems to transfer online. *Student feel they must maintain a perfect, happy veneer on Facebook and other profiles attached to their names. They must be that high-achieving, do-no-wrong, unstoppable, successful young woman or man with whom everyone would be proud to associate, to have as a son or daughter, to boast about as a resident assistant or a member of a team, and, eventually, to hire.* Many students have begun to see what they post (on Facebook, especially) as a chore—a homework assignment to build a happy façade—and even resent such work. Then they "play hard" on sites like Yik Yak where they have learned to unleash, to let go, and often go a bit crazy—even if people get hurt in the process. *They deserve to let loose, after all, since it's tiring to be so perfect all of the time.*[22]

---

20. A more complete presentation of the "youth problem" and responses from both church and society can be found in Bergler, *The Juvenilization of American Christianity*, 20–25.
21. Clark, *Hurt 2.0*, 46.
22. Freitas, *The Happiness Effect*, 12, emphasis added.

Emerging Voices

One can sense the pressure experienced by today's emerging adults and the perception of a lack of support from the culture created by the established generations. Clark argues that this is evident of a larger cultural trend that has devalued the so-called *rite of passage*, traditionally identified through three elements: separation from the old status; transition, usually with a specified ritual; and incorporation into the adult community.[23] Clark argues that more recent cultural dynamics have led to a reality in which "the developmental, societal, and relational needs of children have been neglected . . . and that by the time children reach adolescence they have been left on their own to attempt to navigate the path toward adulthood."[24]

Notice two themes that are apparent in the accounts of adolescents and emerging adults above. First of all, young people believe that they must create their own communities for identity development and genuine connection. David Elkind speaks to this need as a child psychologist saying, "identity formation requires a kind of envelope of adult standards, values and beliefs that the adolescent can confront and challenge in order to construct and test out her own standards, values and beliefs . . . Today, however, adults have fewer standards, values and beliefs and hold on to them less firmly than was true in the past. The adolescent must therefore struggle to find an identity without the benefit of this supportive adult envelope."[25] This means that young people are being forced to create their own communities in which to discover this identity, and are doing it away from the boundaries built on the wisdom of adult experience.

Perhaps this is at least partially to blame for the surge in the amount of stress around the idea of "adulting." Related to this, Jean Twenge, professor of psychology at San Diego State University, noted a marked increase in "maturity fears" in college students today versus those in the 1980s and 1990s.[26] As today's young people transition to adulthood, the standard has shifted and become less defined. Thus, many emerging adults find themselves creating their own supportive communities in order to more clearly dictate the steps necessary for personal development toward maturity.

Secondly, note the limitations emerging adults identify in their ability to create this authentic community through the use of technology. As they describe their online social life, they attach a great deal of pressure to their

---

23. van Gennep, *The Rites of Passage* cited in Clark, *Hurt 2.0*, 7.
24. Clark, *Hurt 2.0*, 8.
25. Elkind, *A Sympathetic Understanding of the Child*, 197.
26. Twenge, *iGen*, 45.

online image. Freitas uncovered a troubling dilemma in her study, which she identifies as "the happiness effect." She identifies the most pressing social media issue in young people as the importance of *appearing* happy. She elaborates, "And not just happy but, as a number of students informed me, blissful, enraptured, even inspiring."[27] This kind of image consciousness reeks of anything but authentic community.

Brandy, a participant in Freitas' study, sums up this issue well as she identifies what she calls the "reputation self." She says, "The way you want people to see you [online] isn't a true reflection of yourself but that's still a *version* of yourself."[28] Any person seeking authentic community must know that presenting a *version* of yourself is not sufficient. However, Brandy' concern speaks to another internal effect of today's technological world: anxiety.

Twenge gives a troubling overview of the connection between screens and mental health in her book, *iGen*. In this study she consults results from Monitoring the Future, an ongoing study of American youth that originated in 1975, and she sees a well-defined trend:

> The results could not be clearer: teens who spend more time on screen activities are more likely to be unhappy, and those who spend more time on nonscreen activities are more likely to be happy. There's not a single exception: all screen activities are linked to less happiness, and all nonscreen activities are linked to more happiness.[29]

Although Twenge is careful to limit causation versus correlation when it comes to technology's relationship to anxiety, more and more studies are beginning to suspect that greater use of technology is at least partially to blame for the increase of anxiety in emerging adults.[30] The Barna Group's research on Generation Z notes that this generation lives their social life on their phones and that much more of their time than in previous generations is spent "in their room, alone and often distressed."[31]

Some of this can be explained by the now familiar acronym FOMO, or fear of missing out: "Those who aren't invited are keenly aware, through social media, of what is happening without them, leading to feelings of exclusion and loneliness. Those who post are also affected, anxiously waiting

---

27. Freitas, *The Happiness Effect*, 13.
28. Freitas, *The Happiness Effect*, 73.
29. Twenge, *iGen*, 77–78.
30. Twenge, *iGen*, 77–81.
31. *Gen Z*, Barna Group, 16.

for the affirmation of comments and 'likes.'"[32] Twenge explains it this way: "[Social life] is conducted online, for all to see, with clear messages about who's in and who's out."[33]

The reality of one's social existence online is key to understand when it comes to emerging adulthood. As new forms of social media have been introduced over the last several years, today's emerging adult lives in a world where they have always performed in front of an online audience. In their teens, Facebook, YouTube, Wikipedia, and Twitter were introduced and iPhones placed access to these tools in the palms of their hands. By the time they reached late adolescence, smartphones and tablets were ubiquitous and were used for everything from browsing the internet to texting to media access, all while maintaining continual connectivity to one's online community. Some studies have estimated that the average emerging adult in America interacts with screens for up to twelve hours a day, with social media occupying an hour of that time.[34]

In *The Culture of Connectivity: A Critical History of Social Media*, Jose Van Djick identifies what she calls the "popularity principle" as a social media concept where quantity equals value. Van Djick says, "Online quantification indiscriminately accumulates acclamation and applause, and, by implication, deprecation and disapproval. Popularity . . . thus not only becomes quantifiable but also manipulatable: boosting popularity rankings is an important mechanism built into these buttons."[35] It is no wonder that an emerging adult's phone yields so much power over their internal life.

External Effects

This leads to the second family of effects digital communication has had on emerging adults, namely the external effects. In a sense, the external effects of today's technological world cause a sort of cyclical effect. As emerging adults live out their lives online, they share with technology a *version* of themselves (remember Brandy above) to which technology capitulates and feeds them more resources to build this image. As emerging adults encounter this reality based off of a less-than-true version of themselves, they respond likewise.

32. *Gen Z*, Barna Group, 19.
33. Twenge, *iGen*, 54.
34. Arnett, *Emerging Adulthood*, 196.
35. Van Djick, *The Culture of Connectivity*, 13.

Screens Disciple

The Algorithm

The idea of the algorithm which directs our digital lives is one that has been in the news in recent years, as companies such as Google, Facebook, and Twitter have dealt with various concerns related to their control over an individual's access to information. No matter one's position on the role of these systems it can be agreed that the effect of technology on the information that one takes in influences how they see the world around them. Turkle puts it this way: "The system presents us with what it believes we will buy or read or vote for. It places us in a particular world that constrains our sense of what is out there and what is possible."[36] Technology shapes how one sees the world to the extent that it controls the world which one sees. Soon, if one is not careful, it is easy to narrow one's exposure to ideas they already know. Or perhaps more concerning, to ideas they already like.

This algorithm, though, has contributed to a new phenomenon in emerging adulthood: an emphasis on safety, particularly *emotional* safety. Twenge notes that this emphasis has led to a rather surprising conclusion: "the idea that one should be safe not just from car accidents and sexual assault but from people who disagree with you."[37] Greg Lukianoff, president of the Foundation for Individual Rights in Education, and Jonathan Haidt, professor of ethical leadership at New York University's Stern School of Business see this as a shift to a subjective standard. In their book *The Coddling of the American Mind* they note that trauma, bullying, and abuse for the average college student are not objectively defined but based off of the individual's emotional response.[38] Twenge quotes Northwestern University professor, Laura Kipnis: "Emotional discomfort is [now] regarded as equivalent to material injury, and all injuries have to be remediated."[39] Ideas that disagree with one's point of view, then, border closely—or even cross the line into—the notion of assault.

Perhaps this is why some emerging adults speak almost idyllically about the idea of avoiding controversy online. In Sherry Turkle's interviews with college students, one particular student demonstrates this by saying, she "is glad not to have anything controversial on [her] mind, because [she]

---

36. Turkle, *Reclaiming Conversation*, 307.
37. Twenge, *iGen*, 154.
38. Lukianoff and Haidt, *The Coddling of the American Mind*, 26.
39. Twenge, *iGen*, 156.

can't think of an online place where it would be safe to have controversial conversations."[40] Turkle explains the student's position further:

> She would want to have any conversation online because that is where she is in touch with all her friends. [But she] describes a circle that encourages silence: If she had controversial opinions she would express them online, so it's good that she has none, because what she would say would not be private in this medium. In fact, [her] circle has one more reinforcing turn: She says it's good that she has nothing controversial to say because she would be saying it online and everything you say online is kept forever. And that is something that she doesn't like at all.[41]

Freitas' study, *The Happiness Effect*, demonstrates similar results. In a particular instance, one of Freitas' study participants describes this understanding from her perspective: "If everyone plays along and pretends that all is well, then the 'audience' gets to feel at ease, even apathetic, about everything they see . . . passive viewers, scrolling through the feed and nodding their heads and never really having to engage anyone on a level that is real."[42] The audience is once again front and center; however, this time the concern is not so much based on vulnerability, but the responsibility of one to another to share in a way that is not bothersome to others.

This idea of an audience came up often in Freitas' study with college students. She says, "Several wrote that online image is important to think about because you have to consider the 'audience' you are reaching; one of these students went so far as to say that 'you pick a target audience (sometimes unconsciously) and you curate. You form your image and identity around whomever you're trying to please.'"[43] Once again, one can hear the internal anxiety of emerging adults in connection with social media; however, this image curation transitions from internal to external once it is recognized how this effects their online communication. *You form your image and identity around whomever you're trying to please.*

Take for example a 2014 study that demonstrates that American college students who declare themselves as either committed Republicans or Democrats intentionally avoid political discussion with fellow students

---

40. Turkle, *Reclaiming Conversation*, 311.
41. Turkle, *Reclaiming Conversation*, 311.
42. Freitas, *The Happiness Effect*, 68.
43. Freitas, *The Happiness Effect*, 71.

who do not share their political views.⁴⁴ A Pew Research Center study characterizes this dynamic as a "spiral of silence." They say, "People don't want to post opinions on social media that they fear their followers will disagree with ... People use the Internet to limit their interactions to those with whom they agree. And social media users are less willing than non-users to discuss their views off-line."⁴⁵ The promise of interfacing with a broader range of ideas in the digital age seems to be a myth.

#Activism

This is not to say, however, that today's emerging adults are completely unwilling to discuss anything of substance online. Turkle reviews the #StopKony online initiative in 2012 in which a group called Invisible Children sought to bring awareness and an end to the militant regime of Joseph Kony in central Africa. The online campaign garnered tremendous support only to fizzle as mouse clicks were set to transition to active participation. Turkle describes the campaign as a "friendship model" of political action where "we friend, we share, and those in political power ultimately surrender."⁴⁶ The lesson of #StopKony was a lesson of strong ties (people you know and trust) versus weak ties (friends of friends or casual acquaintances): "[Weak ties] are good for getting people talking but not effective in getting them to do much else. [People were] intoxicated by the feeling of being part of a vibrant and growing movement. But the website couldn't get people to put real signs on real lawns. It couldn't get people to declare themselves to their physical neighbors."⁴⁷ It seems that hashtags are better for collecting likes than they are for starting a revolution.⁴⁸

---

44. Turkle-Willard, "The Irrelevant Opposition: Reference Groups in the Formation of Political Attitudes Among Partisan College Students," 322.

45. Hampton et al., "Social Media and the 'Spiral of Silence,'" as cited in Turkle, *Reclaiming Conversation*, 322.

46. Turkle, *Reclaiming Conversation*, 296.

47. Turkle, *Reclaiming Conversation*, 296–97.

48. It should be noted that there are proponents of this kind of activism. For example, Shirky, *Here Comes Everybody*. Advocates such as Shirky point to the #StopKony campaign as a failure of one organization to incite true change, rather than giving in to the broader vision of "slacktivism" (the feeling of activism rather than the true act) that critics cite regarding online activism.

In fact, in weak tie relationships the basic rule is to ask little.[49] But think about this in relation to what has been covered regarding the online image of emerging adults. If one's image is to be carefully curated and managed in a way that is sure not to raise controversy, then real activism would seem to be limited. Instead, it seems more likely that activism would be tied to popular movements and initiatives that temper risk and *help* in building one's online image.

Hashtag activism is not only unhelpful in many cases, it can be detrimental, particularly in its failure to bring about the kind of conversations that lead to heart change regarding such issues.[50] Theological campuses who seek to raise up young people to carry the flag of Christianity into the next generation must seek ways to go deeper than #activism, especially when it comes to proclaiming their faith.

Conclusion

All of this points to a general reality that emerging adults' relationship to their screens have influenced their willingness to proclaim their faith. Kinnaman and Matlock note that in much online interaction snarky and sarcastic rule the day over earnest and sincere,[51] which makes for a difficult space when it comes to sharing faith. Turkle makes a similar argument regarding the current state of political discourse. She says, "There is a lot of conversation—both online and off—in which opponents broadcast prepared sound bites. There is a lot of staged conversation. You can avoid challenging conversations on and off the web. The web just makes it easier."[52] Neither of these approaches encourage the kind of authentic conversations which lead to true heart change. Technology has changed the way the world

---

49. Gladwell, "Small Change: Why the Revolution Will Not Be Tweeted," as cited in Turkle, *Reclaiming Conversation*, 297.

50. As I was completing this project, two particular social movements began to change the perspective regarding online activism. Beginning in 2017, the #MeToo movement arose on behalf of women who had been sexually harassed. Then, during the writing of this project, #BlackLivesMatter grew exponentially in the wake of the killing of George Floyd at the hands of Minneapolis police officers. As more objective research is completed on these movements and how they motivated people beyond keystrokes toward tangible action, these might provide a useful example for leading through online activism.

51. Kinnaman and Matlock, *Faith for Exiles*, 27.

52. Turkle, *Reclaiming Conversation*, 298.

communicates and has introduced new hurdles, even as it promises to tear others down. Particularly, this is true in arenas of intimate discussion, as in the area of faith proclamation. In short, *screens disciple*.

Although the challenge of proclaiming the good news of Christ in the current age is palpable, the charge remains the same. This means that those who take seriously the task of passing on the faith must look for ways to engage emerging adults and to call them to a higher purpose—a mission. Theological higher education is key to this task and, as campuses seek to raise up a new generation of Christian leaders, they must do so with an eye toward proclamation in the twenty-first century. The next chapter will seek to address these challenges.

5

An Analog Response

As I WAS BEGINNING my research for the previous chapter, attempting to understand the effect of screens on emerging adults' ability to proclaim their faith, I was approached by a college administrator inquiring about my research. As I briefly described the work I had been doing, he asked if I would be willing to present my findings as his institution worked to develop a technology policy in light of changes to higher education brought on by the COVID-19 pandemic. Although I was fully in support of what he was trying to do, I also knew that my research was less about how to use technology than it was about circumventing its negative effects. This is not to say that my intention is to demonize technology, but that the response to its effects would need to look more like a set of disciplines than a new digital strategy.

Analog: Not Digital; Not Computerized

In light of this reality, the responses below focus on the analog response of the theological campus. Analog, as defined by Merriam Webster's dictionary, means "not digital; not computerized."[1] To overcome the challenges presented above, the theological campus must fashion a response that lies outside of the boundaries of the common technological worldview of emerging adulthood. That does not mean a rejection of technology, but rather a holistic response that speaks to the entirety of the person and the effects of

---

1. https://www.merriam-webster.com/dictionary/analog

the technological world in which they live. The theological campus must recognize that these effects are all-encompassing, leaving a lasting mark on both the internal and external world of the emerging adult. Below are a few strategies that the theological campus must employ in their response.

Giving Support; Giving Space

As emerging adults are faced with a world of ever-growing complexity, we have already noted the correlation to a demonstrable rise in anxiety. It is important that emerging adults be surrounded by caring adults who demonstrate their support in two ways. First, they must be willing to give emerging adults support as they grow into maturity. This implies a certain level of empathy. Note that empathy is not the same as sympathy. Stanford University's "D" School defines empathizing as "the work you do to understand people . . . It is your effort to understand the way they do things and why, their physical and emotional needs, how they think about the world, and what is meaningful to them."[2] Empathy is seeking to walk in understanding alongside of another.[3]

Second, caring adults need to learn to give space to emerging adults as they transition into maturity, seeking to connect while respecting proper boundaries. Corey Seemiller and Meghan Grace have adapted years of experience in working with college students into a helpful guide entitled *Generation Z Goes to College*. In this text, the authors describe many of the complexities of the current generation of emerging adults and how colleges can come alongside of them in this time of development. Related to digital communication, Seemiller and Grace describe social media outlets such as Twitter, Instagram, and Snapchat as "authority-figure-free zones"[4] and warn adults of the "creepy tree house" where "adults and authority figures enter the social networking space that was previously used for peers to

---

2. Powell et al., *Growing Young*, 91–92.

3. It ought to be no surprise that empathy was one of the top factors identified by young people, including emerging adults, in the Churches Engaging Young People (CEYP, pronounced "keep") study done by Fuller Youth Institute (FYI) from 2012–2015. Of all of the factors noted in this study, which included online surveys of more than 250 churches more than 10,000 pages of interview with over 500 young people, empathy was one of the six that mentioned often enough for FYI to highlight in their findings. More information on the CEYP study can be found at https://churchesgrowingyoung.com/wp-content/uploads/2016/09/Growing-Young-Research-Method-1.pdf.

4. Seemiller and Grace, *Generation Z Goes to College*, 80.

connect with each other."⁵ The principle that theological colleges must recognize is that emerging adults need a place to *emerge* apart from critical adult eyes. Of course, most theological campuses must employ a level of oversight in light of Christian lifestyle expectations, but staff and faculty should be challenged to navigate these spaces with wisdom as they disciple young people toward a fuller expression of their Christian faith.

Genuine Community

Key to this is that emerging adults need genuine community in which to experience these pivotal years of life. As digital communication tempts to curate a false self, emerging adults need a community of support that honors their personhood. This kind of community does not demand a complete unplugging from digital communication, but an emphasis on authentic communication and participation.

Turkle speaks to something similar when she speaks of the difference between a consumer and a citizen. A consumer is able to consume goods, but at a cost, while a citizen is an active participant and is rewarded as the community is strengthened. Turkle says, "It seems that by agreeing to be a consumer you gave away rights that you might want to claim as a citizen."⁶ The consumer relationship reflects something similar to what Dean describes as a relationship that is "something that we do *to* others in order to get them to do what we want them to do."⁷ Especially as emerging adults enter a markedly optimistic time in one's development,⁸ they demonstrate a great deal of introspection about their relationships and this sort of transactional relationship will not suffice. Those seeking to build genuine community with emerging adults must demonstrate fidelity, or "even if"⁹ relationships, as they model unconditional love. Especially in a technological world that has effectively quantified relationships, the theological campus must re-think how it views community in the face of a culture that has become fascinated by accomplishment.

---

5. Seemiller and Grace, *Generation Z Goes to College*, 223.
6. Turkle, *Reclaiming Conversation*, 327.
7. Dean et al., *Delighted*, 23.
8. Arnett, *Emerging Adulthood*, 309.
9. Dean et al., *Delighted*, 27.

An Analog Response

Be the Fire and Wish for the Wind!

Similarly, the theological campus must reconsider its objectives, recognizing that education in a theological sense is formational more than it is informational. Although it is my impression that many in theological higher education already share this belief, the impetus is on the campus to reflect this in a way that *students* come to a full belief in this. We have already discussed the culture of achievement and how this has led to a sense of adult abandonment, but research indicates that students studying for vocational ministry—presumably raised in youth group—have a particular attachment to this kind of "works righteousness" in their relationship with Christian adults in their lives.[10] Theological faculty and staff must represent a fresh new wind that blows into the lives of students, as they challenge them to new heights while also promising to be there through the highs and lows.

This speaks directly to the level of anxiety that has come to be associated with emerging adults' usage of technology. The theological campus must renew its commitment to placing challenges in front of students and celebrating with them as they overcome. This practice must cultivate in students a concept akin to the idea of antifragility proposed by New York University professor, Nassim Nicholas Taleb, in his book *Antifragile*. Taleb notes the difference between something like a teacup that is fragile and can break easily and something like a plastic cup that is resilient and can withstand shock. But then he introduces a lesser known category, that of objects that are *antifragile*. These "become rigid, weak, and inefficient when nothing challenges them or pushes them to respond vigorously."[11] Taleb notes examples such as muscles, bones, and children as being antifragile.

Taleb speaks about this topic with poetic flare, inviting adults in the lives of young people to ignite them in an entirely new way. He challenges them, "You want to be the fire and wish for the wind."[12] A challenge such as this speaks to the relationship between adult mentors, professors, as well as other influencers and their relationship to the emerging adults around them. Although we empathize with their plight, as mentioned above, we seek to push them to new heights, particularly in recognizing their potential for proclaiming the gospel in a way which can speak to their culture.

---

10. Dean et al., *Delighted*, 35–36.

11. Taleb, *Antifragile* as cited in Lukianoff and Haidt, *The Coddling of the American Mind*, 23.

12. As quoted in Lukianoff and Haidt, *The Coddling of the American Mind*, 23.

Ironically, this approach pushes emerging adults toward a new level of freedom. As Dean puts it, a relationship that is "freely and voluntarily chosen, *regardless of the potential or lack of potential for reciprocity.*"[13] This opens the door for students to experience the freedom of a covenantal friendship rather than the bondage of a transactional relationship. This not only changes their campus experience, but it changes their perspective on adult relationships.

Lukianoff and Haidt, in *The Coddling of the American Mind*, propose an approach to teaching antifragility which incorporates the basic tenets of their therapeutic method, cognitive behavior therapy. Cognitive behavior therapy employs, among others things, the A-B-C theory behind Albert Ellis' Rational Emotive Behavioral Therapy. Ellis recognized that people often attribute behavioral or emotional consequences to some activating event (A). REBT recognizes that people are not most disturbed by the event, however, but by the beliefs (B) which they hold about the event which led to the consequent emotions (C) for which the client is often seeking counsel. The job of the therapist in this model, then, is to teach clients how to respond to what Ellis recognized as inaccurate beliefs which led to their depleted emotional state. The response that Ellis taught was to dispute (D) these inaccurate beliefs, often called cognitive distortions, in order to work toward a more positive cognitive effect (E).[14] In essence, a cognitive response such as this motivates one toward an antifragile approach to life's difficulties.

This speaks to a key formational piece that appears to be lacking, as Twenge notes that many emerging adults feel increasingly demoralized in our achievement culture. In psychology this points to an external locus of control, meaning that one believes their life is controlled by outside sources. Someone with an internal locus of control, on the other hand, believes they are the ones in control of their life. Many in this generation are being identified with an external locus of control, as those studying them recognize a belief that they have little control over the outcome of their life.[15] Helping them to clear hurdles through their own strength and determination, and then celebrating each victory along the way is a way to build the kind of antifragility and belief in an internal locus of control that is vital for emerging adults transitioning into a challenging adult world.

---

13. Dean et al., *Delighted*, 33.
14. Jones and Butman, *Modern Psychotherapies*, 214.
15. Twenge, *iGen*, 191.

An Analog Response

Nowhere could this be more important than in the area of their faith proclamation. As we have already seen, emerging adults find it more difficult to share their faith online, citing concerns about how this will be perceived in the "in or out" world of social media. Perhaps the greatest tool the theological campus has in changing this trend is to raise up young ministers who understand faith proclamation as something more than a statement and rather as a walk in which they are strengthened by the support around them. Faith proclamation must become less about making the right statement (which, it must be admitted, carries a level of anxiety in itself) and more about living a life of faith accompanied by an ability to proclaim what Jesus Christ has done in one's life. As budding ministers find themselves put into situations where they are challenged to share their faith in this way, they will find freedom in the expression of their faith.

Break the Algorithm

In order to find this freedom, though, students in the digital age need to be pushed to expand their perspective. As digital technologies seek to shrink the world of emerging adults, theological educators need to seek to expand their worldview by exposing them to difficult questions and conversations. It is ironic that this generation is becoming synonymous with the online echo chamber while they are surrounded by more diversity than any previous generation in American history.[16] Unfortunately, as the information above has proven, diversity is not enough to open one's mind.

As we noted in the previous chapter, our screens are designed to feed us the information which we most relate to and, more dangerously, which we *like*. In *12 Ways Your Phone Is Changing You*, Reinke captures the danger of this reality: "The object of our *worship* is the object of our *imitation*. God designed this inseparable pattern. What we want to become, we worship. And what we worship shapes our becoming."[17] Emerging adults live in a world that is increasingly designed to feed into a level of narcissism, even to the point of self-worship. And the statistics shared previously demonstrate what a dead-end destination this has proven to be.

Emerging adults need adult mentors who are willing to challenge them to look beyond their limited worldview. As theologian David Wells warns of this limited perspective, "The biblical interest in righteousness is

---

16. *Gen Z*, 29–34.
17. Reinke, *12 Ways Your Phone Is Changing You*, 113.

replaced by a search for happiness, holiness by wholeness, truth by feeling, ethics by feeling good about one's self. The world shrinks to the range of personal circumstances; the community of faith shrinks to a circle of personal friends. The past recedes. The Church recedes. The world recedes. All that remains is the self."[18] The theological campus must be a place that challenges this worldview and seeks for opportunities in which to expose students to realities beyond those seen on their phone. This speaks to their own faith maturity, but also to their ability to proclaim this faith to others.

True Activism

Lastly, emerging adults need a campus community that will help them to discover true activism. Theological education must not shy away from emerging adults' desire for social justice. This means that they need to be exposed to injustice in the world and be allowed to formulate a response. This also means that theological educators must not shy away from the demonstrated desire in emerging adults to address these concerns.[19] Students stepping into ministry in the twenty-first century must be informed and prepared to face the world in which they live, not the world about which many evangelicals reminisce. There are already communities of emerging adults gathering around this mission,[20] and theological educators must recognize that increasingly emerging adults do not identify the church as truly operating in its mission if it is not speaking to justice in the world. Faculty must use their classrooms and staff and administration must use their offices to point out injustice and to act biblically on behalf of the downtrodden.

This also means that authentic discourse must be allowed on sensitive issues within contemporary culture. Kinnaman notes that one of the main reasons behind the loss of young people from our congregations is that the church has not honestly dealt with the complexity of the contemporary

---

18. As quoted in Detweiler, *Selfies*, 135.
19. Powell et al., *Growing Young*, 234–67.
20. One in particular is the "& Campaign" which states: "As Christians, we are called to civic and community engagement. We have a duty to impact culture in a manner that reflects the truth (&) love of Jesus Christ. This commission includes participation in the political arena, wherein actions or inaction can have a profound effect on all aspects of society. Life, freedom and the general well-being of all citizens can be significantly enhanced or diminished by political dynamics." https://andcampaign.org/about-1.

world.²¹ Students preparing for ministry in the current cultural climate must be prepared to facilitate such discussions or the church runs the risk of becoming irrelevant to an entire generation. If the theological campus can grasp the importance of this issue and harness the desire of this generation to put Jesus' gospel plan into action, the church of the twenty-first century will be in good hands. As students learn the art of speaking their minds in a secure environment, they will develop confidence and boldness to proclaim their faith in ways which speak to this generation and to communicate their faith in both word and in deed.

Conclusion

As I said at the beginning of this chapter, this response is less about fashioning a new technological approach as it is a return to a set of disciplines. As the theological campus commits itself to the principles above, it opens the door to the kind of relationships between adults and emerging adults that can lead the church into the best form of ministry for the twenty-first century.

At the core of this idea is a re-definition of the adult/emerging adult relationship. Modern thought around friendship centers around the concepts of mutuality and reciprocity, a line of thought put forward by Aristotle. John Swinton, chair in divinity and religious studies at the School of Divinity, History, and Philosophy at the University of Aberdeen, calls it "the principle of likeness."²² It is at least partially to this understanding that our culture owes its generational divide in relationships; in any relationship where "likeness" is impossible, intimacy is not realistic. However, as the theologian Jürgen Moltmann says, "only someone who finds the courage to be different from others can ultimately exist for 'others.'"²³ As Dean puts it, "It's not 'social difference' that needs to be minimized; it's 'social distance.'"²⁴

This is especially true in the age of the algorithm, as technology plays the gatekeeper for the information that an emerging adult is exposed to. Adults who recognize their difference and how to use this distance to challenge students to broaden their understanding of the world—especially as they engage Scripture together—have the opportunity to open the door to

---

21. Kinnaman, *You Lost Me*, 98.
22. Swinton, *From Bedlam to Shalom*, 84–86 as cited in Dean et al., *Delighted*, 32–33.
23. Jürgen Moltmann, *The Crucified God*, 16 as cited in Dean et al., *Delighted*, 33.
24. Dean et al., *Delighted*, 33.

a new and hopeful life. Dean describes this potential as she connects the concept of freedom to joy:

> This freedom, in fact, is why friendship is so closely linked to *joy*, because joy also has freedom at its heart. Joy is essentially about delighting in God and, more importantly, enjoying God's delight in us. Friendship is what joy looks like in the form of a relationship. It is enduring because it is rooted in delight and, therefore, necessarily noninstrumental.[25]

As staff and faculty seek relationships with students that are less instrumental—more covenantal than contractual—they stand the chance of empowering a generation to minister to a culture that is less and less familiar to those beyond the years of emerging adulthood. As students find fidelity in these relationships, they will find freedom in discovering and expressing their faith. And suddenly screens will have an entirely new potential to disciple a generation for Christ.

---

25. Dean et al., *Delighted*, 33.

6

Exiles in Training

IN ORDER TO CLARIFY the role of the theological campus in reclaiming the Christian language, a particular theological lens might be helpful. As the average Christian emerging adult stands on the outskirts of Western contemporary culture, one might see them as functioning in an exilic reality. As was outlined previously, the predominant view of this culture places one who sees Christian faith as anything more than subjective personal values on the margins of society. This means that Christian emerging adults live as functional exiles in an unfriendly culture.[1] As such, the following chapter lays out an exilic understanding of the role of the theological campus in contemporary culture, especially in reclaiming the Christian language.

Framing the Discussion on Exile

The issue of exile has been an area of concern in the Judeo-Christian history dating back to as early as the captivity of Israel in Egypt. However, this matter has once again risen to prominence through the work of notable New Testament scholar, N. T. Wright, and his "continuing exile" thesis.[2] In

---

1. For an early proposal of the church's reaction to such an "alien" culture see Hauerwas and Willimon. *Resident Aliens*.

2. Originally proposed in Wright, *Paul and the Faithfulness of God*, and further unpacked in response to many of the common rebuttals to his theory in Wright, "Yet the Sun Will Rise Again." ed. by Scott.

this theory,[3] Wright recognizes a theme of continuing exile in Israel all the way up to the point of Jesus breaking through with the new hope for which Israel had longed.[4] Wright seeks to accomplish this task through what he calls a history of theology, which recognizes that history and theology must be "mutually interdependent ways of talking about the same thing."[5] Wright, then, specifically examines how history demonstrates Israel's vision of God as well as His work in and through and also His sovereignty over the events of history. A brief overview of Wright's thesis, although doing little to suggest contemporary application,[6] is helpful in being able to engage the contemporary research surrounding the topic.

Metaphorically Speaking

In Jesus, Wright sees one who intended to "remake the people of God"[7] and to fulfill the hope that Israel was intended to bring through his messiahship. Wright presents the Hebrew Scripture as "a story in search of an ending,"[8] and that this fulfilment is found in Christ.[9] Specifically, Wright sees in the writings of the Apostle Paul that this period of exile has come to an end through the work of Christ.[10] Wright's theory is certainly not without critics.[11]

---

3. Michael F. Bird notes that "This proposal is not altogether novel and it bears a resemblance to earlier works by Odil Steck, Paul Garnet, Mark Knibb, James M. Scott, and others, in relation to their investigation of exile in the Hebrew Bible and Second Temple Jewish literature." Bird, "Jesus and the Continuing Exile of Israel in the Writings of N.T. Wright."

4. Wright's "Continuing Exile" theory serves as an extension of the discussion on restoration eschatology initiated in Sanders, *Jesus and Judaism*.

5. Wright, "Yet the Sun Will Rise Again," 72.

6. This same dissatisfaction is expressed by others throughout *Exile: A Conversation with N.T. Wright*, ed. by James Scott, 2017.

7. Wright, "Yet the Sun Will Rise Again," 48.

8. Wright, *Paul and the Faithfulness of God*, 109.

9. "The Creator/covenant God has brought his covenant purpose for Israel to fruition in *Israel's representative, the Messiah, Jesus. Therefore, now, a new world has dawned.* The new day promised by the prophets, and by Moses himself in Deuteronomy, has arrived." Wright, "Yet the Sun Will Rise Again," 62.

10. Wright, "Yet the Sun Will Rise Again," 62.

11. For a thorough list of both critics and supporters of Wright's "continuing exile" theory, see Bird, "Jesus and the Continuing Exile of Israel in the Writings of N. T. Wright."

Exiles in Training

In this theory, though, Wright makes it clear that he does not see this as a metaphorical image but strictly as historical experience:

> The main point about narratives in the second-Temple Jewish world, and in that of Paul, is not simply that people liked telling stories as illustrations of, or scriptural proofs for, this or that experience or doctrine, but rather that second-Temple Jews believed themselves to be *actors within* a real-life narrative.[12]

This meant that Israel in the time of Jesus lived in a sense of continuing exile in which they proceeded to search for the hope that had been promised them, a "grand narrative" that Wright sees behind Jesus' teaching throughout the gospels.[13] This promise would only be fulfilled once all was set back in right standing, and Wright believes this had happened in Jesus' death: "The point was that, if sins were forgiven, the exile would be over, the rule of the evil powers would be broken, and Israel—and the rest of the world—would be summoned to enjoy, and to take part in, God's renewed world."[14] This is exactly what Paul sees as being fulfilled in the death of Jesus and thus as the conclusion to Israel's exilic struggle, and indeed as the means that the whole human race is rescued from exile.[15] In Wright's eyes, as Jesus proclaimed "kingdom stories" and as Paul examines Jesus' work from an eschatological standpoint, the fulfillment of this vision is apparent. Israel's God had promised a new day for His people, that "one day the sun would rise at last."[16] In Jesus' crucifixion, resurrection, and reign, He had fulfilled his promise.[17]

---

12. Wright, *Paul and the Faithfulness of God*, 114.

13. Bird points out the problematic sense of such a grand narrative behind Jesus' parables and teachings. "Although many of the parables are stories of Israel in miniature (e.g. Mk. 4.1–34), they focus not on return from exile, but more generally with the notion of 'God, God's people, and God's word.'" Bird, "Jesus and the Continuing Exile of Israel in the Writings of N. T. Wright."

14. Wright, "Yet the Sun Will Rise Again," 68.

15. Wright, "Yet the Sun Will Rise Again," 71.

16. Wright, "Yet the Sun Will Rise Again," 80.

17. Steven M. Bryan offers what would seem to summarize the predominant argument against Wright: "The exile, then, should not be thought an invariable aspect of Israel's ongoing self-awareness. Wright is certainly correct to perceive a wide-spread awareness of bondage and belief that the promises of restoration had not yet been fulfilled, but to extrapolate from this a corresponding belief that the exile was ongoing serves only to distort the complex history of Israel and its interpretation within Second Temple Judaism, as well as key elements of the Jesus tradition." Bryan, "Jesus and Israel's Eschatological Constitution."

Although Wright's recent publications have done much to bring the topic of exile back to the forefront of biblical studies, his rejection of a metaphoric view of exile[18] makes his theory difficult to apply to a study of twenty-first-century emerging adults. For this reason, Brueggemann, a key biblical scholar in the area of exile, finds Wright unsatisfactory in application and feels as though his conclusion leaves much work for the contemporary church.[19] We will attempt here to make this connection.

Contemporary Exiles

As has been explained earlier in this paper, the secular view of the twenty-first century firmly places any emerging adult with a Christian worldview on the margins of mainstream culture. With this in mind, we will proceed with the theological and biblical basis for the current age in which emerging adults live, assessed through the eyes of the biblical exile: people of faith on the margins of society.

Through a closer look at this biblical—and indeed historical—Judeo-Christian identity, one can surmise both what these groups did for survival and in carrying on the proclamation of the message of God. This exilic community will be examined from this point forward through the metaphorical lens of Brueggemann[20]—that of biblical studies informing contemporary praxis. Brueggemann proposes that "the Old Testament experience of and reflection upon exile is a helpful *metaphor* for understanding our current faith situation in the U.S. church, and a *model* for pondering new forms of ecclesiology."[21] Although this metaphor has been engaged at different points in time,[22] Brueggemann's illustration remains the foundation on which most "contemporary church as exile" arguments are based.

Our next task, then is to examine the usefulness of a lens which establishes a connection between the biblical image of the exile and that of

18. Wright, *Paul and the Faithfulness of God*, 21.

19. Brueggemann, "Wright on Exile: A Response," 90.

20. This metaphorical view differs from Wright's "continuing exile" motif and, in fact, Brueggemann takes issue with Wright's lack of contemporary application of his theory in Brueggemann, "Wright on Exile, 90: "Surely Wright is correct on his tilt in these matters. But his articulation still lingers in a rather abstract way. He leaves much more work to do about the matter of exile in contemporary life."

21. Brueggemann, *Cadences of Home*, 1, emphasis original.

22. I.e., Frost, *Exiles, Exilic Preaching*, ed. by Clarke, as well as various essays throughout *Exile*, ed. by Scott.

Exiles in Training

the emerging adult Christian in twenty-first century Western culture. Once these connections have been established, the attention will shift toward a re-establishment of Christian identity through the use of language which can be encouraged by the theological campus.

Students as Exiles

Brueggemann identifies two facets of the exilic period of ancient Israel: Little influence over public policy and temptations toward cultural syncretism.[23] These facets help us to recognize the metaphorical correlation between emerging adults in the twenty-first century and the exilic Israel of the Old Testament.

First of all, Brueggemann makes the point that exiles have little influence over public policy. Ancient Israel found itself bound to the laws and culture of those who held power over them, whether it be the Babylonians, the Persians, or as more recent scholarship suggests, in Israel's state under Rome.[24] In all of these cases, Israel had become "politically innocuous and irrelevant"[25] and thus history records a tellingly one-sided tale of power and influence.[26]

It is no stretch to recognize the state of contemporary Western Christianity in this exilic metaphor as what many perceive to be "innocuous and irrelevant" in an increasingly secular society. Some might say that Western

---

23. Brueggemann, *Cadences of Home*, 104–5.
24. Wright, *Paul and the Faithfulness of God*, 177.
25. Brueggemann, *Cadences of Home*, 104.

26. It is notable that in Kieffer, "Not All Gloom and Doom," 123–25, the argument is made that an emotional valuation of Israel's displacement is out of place. Kieffer's argument specifically examines the words הָלֹוג (*golah*) and תּוּלָג (*galut*) as the common Hebrew for "exile" and reminds biblical readers that neither implies a valuation of the term. Although contemporary English translations introduce these kinds of nuances into the text, Kieffer warns that one should be careful that not to assign a deeper emotional concept to exiled Israel than is necessary. Point in case, Kieffer references a rabbinic commentary on the Hebrew Scripture, the *Mekhilta*, which "makes the bold claim that when the Israelites had to leave their homeland, God himself went into exile with them." His thesis is that distance from their former home did not equate to distance from their God. An exile was not hopeless, even in their displacement, and one should be careful not to recognize this valuation unnecessarily. Kieffer's thrust seems to be in defending against an overly emotional attachment to these circumstances, but not in an overall understanding of the challenges presented in exile, as are most important to the purposes of this paper.

emerging adults have never known anything different; their Christian faith has always been marginal at best when it comes to influencing their culture. Certain religious scholars point to the role of the church in its inability to communicate its core truths[27] and, in fact, the researchers behind the National Study of Youth and Religion (NSYR) would agree.[28] However, as has been unpacked already in this paper, there are many factors which have led to the contemporary cultural condition. What is important for our purposes is to recognize the possibility of Christian emerging adults as exiles through their lack of influence over public policy, and how this has impacted their engagement and thus their mastery of the Christian language.

One interesting component of this exilic condition is how the language of a culture both contributes to marginalization and also maintains identity within these circumstances. Philip Alexander notes the intense ideology of the Jewish people and how this stance was "fraught with political consequences."[29] This intense ideology leads to a political thrust that carries through the Jewish history, both marginalizing them but also maintaining their distinction.

However, this otherness is not always easily maintained in exilic conditions. The second facet Brueggemann notes is that exiles face temptations toward cultural syncretism and the disappearance of a characteristic identity. A people's identity is often based heavily in the role and function of public institutions which support the distinction of a given people group. In the state of exile, the displaced people group lacks this kind of public support and are often tempted toward syncretism.[30] Exiles are tempted toward syncretism because their way of life becomes more and more foreign even to them. The more familiar, not to mention socially acceptable, lifestyle becomes that of the foreign culture.

Specific to language, the faith proclamation of exiles takes on a depth that is incomprehensible, and thus offensive and offsetting to the surrounding culture.[31]

27. Dean, *Almost Christian*, 10.

28. Smith, *Soul Searching*, 122.

29. Alexander, "Jewish Nationalism," 138.

30. Brueggeman explains it this way: "Now, because such institutions are lacking, and because the pattern of social payouts tended to invite people away from this community of peculiar identity and passion, the deliberate maintenance of a distinctive identity required great intentionality." Brueggemann, *Cadences of Home*, 104.

31. Robert Altar is noted to have made an observation of the same effect in the opposite direction, as culture affects faith, although still pointing to the centrality of how

A contemporary corollary of this sort of syncretism is systematically unpacked in Bergler's *The Juvenilization of American Christianity*. Bergler sees an historical trend throughout the twentieth century in which American Christianity attempted to stay relevant, but instead found itself enveloped by culture, losing many of its distinctions in the process. Language promoting the faith played a key role in this plunge. Bergler notes one example in the church's history around the time of WWII where young people were continually exposed to rallies that likened "death in service of country" to Christian martyrdom.[32] This kind of religious nationalism has been at play at many times throughout American history,[33] but is perhaps even more evident in its outcome in the current secular age. A seemingly small shift in language has the potential to obliterate the distinguishing marks of a people's identity. It is no coincidence that the NSYR, a study that uncovered just such a loss of religious identity in twenty-first-century America, found in close correlation the inability to articulate one's faith to a lack of clarity even in an understanding of God.[34]

Imagine how easy it is for emerging adults to become syncretized to such a pervasive secular mindset so ingrained in Western culture that it is rarely even recognized. For instance, Christian Smith observes a cultural push toward the desirable quality of "professionalism" as being scientific

---

Christianity must work at identifying and living in the "thickness" of these differences in Willimon, "Postmodern Preaching," 111: "Robert Altar says that, until the parables of Kafka or James Joyce's *Ulysses*, there is a sense in which we modern people had lost the skills necessary to read the Bible. Only after artists were again determined to write reality on a number of levels, exploring the complexities of human consciousness, the mystery of time, the polyvalence of words, were we able to ask the right questions of 1 Kings."

32. Bergler, *The Juvenilization of the American Christianity*, 29.

33. I.e., R. Laurence Moore who argues a sort of civil religion present in some of America's founding fathers, and that it was for them nothing more than a veiled nationalism: "Moreover, religious differences maintained in private, would be in public subordinated to the larger national concern of sustaining moral conduct in the young republic. Jefferson anticipated that within several decades most Americans would be Christians in ethical terms, but no longer much concerned with whether Christ was God, whether he was born of a virgin, or whether he had risen from the dead. If not Deists, they would be Unitarians, the most rational of the then existing forms of Christianity." Moore, *Touchdown Jesus*, 17.

34. Smith's conclusion is telling: "Again, nobody expects adolescents to be sophisticated theologians. But very few of the descriptions of personal beliefs offered by the teenagers we interviewed, especially the Christian teenagers, come close to representing marginally coherent accounts of the basic, important religious beliefs of their own faith traditions. The majority of U.S. teens would badly fail a hypothetical short-answer or essay test of the basic beliefs of their religion." Smith, *Soul Searching*, 137.

and value-free in the late nineteenth and early twentieth centuries. Smith labeled this as nothing short of a "secular revolution," and that "colleges that used to promote 'a general Protestant worldview and morality' were transformed into universities 'where religious concerns were marginalized in favor of the 'objective,' a-religious and irreligious pursuit and transmission of knowledge.'"[35] This seems such a subtle shift and yet its outcome is that religious language no longer has a place in objective conversation, even *professional* conversation. One who chooses to pursue religious discourse is ostracized for what is perceived as subjectivity and closed-mindedness. This mindset is accepted by sociologists,[36] which makes it no wonder that emerging adults have demonstrated such a loss of articulation when it comes to speaking of their faith.[37]

Emerging adults who speak of their faith openly across all issues of their life risk marginalization at best, mockery and dismissal at worst, unless they concede to the cultural pressure to leave their religion behind. Western response to Christianity remains more accommodating than much of the world, however one can see how social standing affects the use of language and thus how this makes it more difficult to establish any distinction in the Christian faith. More dangerous than any level of conscious marginalization, though, is the unconscious reality within most emerging adults that religion simply has no place in the public sphere of conversation.

---

35. Pearcey, *Total Truth*, 98.

36. James Emery White sees it this way in his examination of Generation Z: "Privatization is the process by which a chasm is created between the public and the private spheres of life, and spiritual things are increasingly placed within the private arena. So when it comes to things such as business, politics, or even marriage and the home, personal faith is bracketed off." White, *Meet Generation Z*, 28–29.

37. i.e., Dean, *Almost Christian*, 15–16 where she notes one of the central concerns of the NSYR (and the chief concern of this paper): "Remarkably articulate young people stammered and groped for words when the conversation turned to religion, as if no one had ever asked them these questions before, or as if we were asking questions in another language. Many youth said religion was important, though when pressed they generally could not say how; almost all of them thought religion was a good thing, though most could not describe the difference it made to them personally.;" or Powell et al., *Growing Young*, 133: "Teenagers and emerging adults in America are not devising this tepid faith on their own. They are not substituting moralistic therapeutic deism for the messages they hear and the modeling they see in the churches today. Instead, they are mimicking a tame version of faith that permeates both their churches and their homes. In a fascinating twist, missiologist George Hunter used the exact same phrase, moralistic therapeutic deism (with an added prefix: *consumerist*), to describe the general milieu of *adult* Christianity in America *half a decade before the first NSYR results emerged*."

A Christian faith without confidence in its voice is a disempowered presence in society that is not indicative of the One whom we serve.

Fostering a Response

Recognizing the above facets of exile, their effects and finally their application to the current state of Christian faith in Western culture, it is important to begin to form a way through this situation. Brueggemann notes that exilic communities were forced to develop strategies and mechanisms for survival in order to sustain their identity as a people.[38] In Israel, one can see these strategies developing early on in their history. As Brueggemann notes in a separate work on Israel's model for biblical education: "Every community that wants to last beyond a single generation must concern itself with education."[39] One can recognize in this statement Brueggemann's foresight that Israel, at least as much as any other nation in history, must be concerned with its own fortitude. It is just this kind of response that is needed today when it comes to maintaining a Christian worldview in the midst of contemporary society.

In offering such a response from that of the theological campus, a proposal by Douglas John Hall, Emeritus Professor of Theology at McGill University, is helpful. He says that one must disengage in order to be prepared to reengage with culture, and that such a strategy is not an end in itself but "a strategic matter for the sake of refocusing and redeciding about [one]'s identity and mission."[40] Ironically, this was the common approach of the seminarian and Bible college student of the past; however, it seems that as contemporary culture has infringed more and more on faith matters, pastoral preparation in this manner has become less and less purposefully "disengaged" from the antagonistic culture. It is important to begin with this idea of disengagement before identifying how one can best be prepared to re-engage the culture.

---

38. Brueggemann, *Cadences of Home*, 105.
39. Brueggemann, *The Creative Word*, 1.
40. Brueggemann, *Cadences of Home*, 80.

Emerging Voices

Intentional Disengagement

The danger at this point would be to simply unpack a predictably obtuse and pragmatic argument in support of such a response; however, the atmosphere of the theological campus calls for something more substantial—a realization of the deeper meaning behind such a move. With this aim in mind, let us shift momentarily to one of the key theologians addressing Christian community in the twentieth century, Dietrich Bonhoeffer. Specifically, we will examine how Bonhoeffer's approach relates to such a purposeful disengagement, particularly in the intentional developmental sphere of emerging adulthood.

Bonhoeffer is often recognized for his commitment to Christian community through an emphasis in works such as *Life Together* and *Discipleship*. In these works Bonhoeffer recognizes a deeply theological component within Christian community that community is not idyllic but a divine reality.[41] For instance, he says, "Christian community is not an ideal we have to realize, but rather a reality created by God in Christ in which we may participate."[42] For Bonhoeffer, Christian community was a Christian mandate into which all the church was called to enter.[43]

It is notable for the purposes of this paper that Bonhoeffer spent much of his time in ministry engaging with adolescents and emerging adults. Although one must admit that youth and emerging adults (the latter not yet a recognizable category of human development) in the 1940s would have looked, talked and thought differently than they would today, there remains a comparable situation in Bonhoeffer's ministry. In fact, influential voices in youth ministry today look to Bonhoeffer as an exemplar for what they call the "theological turn" in youth ministry.[44] In sum, it is important for us to remember that one of the most influential theological minds of the twentieth century—and the one to whom we now look in examining this necessarily "disengaged" community—was a minister who likely would

---

41. Bonhoeffer, *Life Together*, 35.

42. Bonhoeffer, *Life Together*, 38.

43. For a classic study on Bonhoeffer's social theology see Green. *Bonhoeffer: A Theology of Sociality.*

44. Andrew Root, speaking for this movement says, "For those of us seeking to make such a turn . . . we stand on the shoulders of Bonhoeffer . . . Dietrich Bonhoeffer is the forefather to the theological turn because he incomparably weaves together youth work, attention to concrete experience and commitment to the revelatory nature of God's continued action in the world through Jesus Christ." Root, *Bonhoeffer as Youth Worker*, 8.

have been most at home in the contemporary worlds of emerging adulthood and theological education.

Community Over Society

Bonhoeffer's quest for Christian community began early in his theological training, dating back to his first doctoral dissertation, *Sanctorum Communio*. Central to this idea of Christian community in Bonhoeffer's mind was the contrast between community and society. In his dissertation, Bonhoeffer draws on the sociological work of Ferdinand Tönnies who contrasts *Gemeinschaft* (community) with *Gesellschaft* (society). Bonhoeffer's thought can be summarized that the Western world has lost its emphasis on community in the escalation of the functional society, and "the fetishizing of productivity."[45] Bonhoeffer follows Tönnies in seeing community as something wholly distinct from society, seeking a church that reflects *Gemeinschaft* over the *Gesellschaft*, "for the *Gemeinschaft* . . . upholds and even creates personhood; the *Gemeinschaft* wears at least some of the stripes of the family."[46] For Bonhoeffer, the church must hold to its identity as community and never give in to the outside pressure of becoming a utilitarian society.

Robert Wilken sees just such an emphasis in Augustine's work on the City of God: "This peace for which the city of God yearns is a 'perfectly ordered and harmonious fellowship in the enjoyment of God,' a peace of 'enjoying one another in God.'"[47] This community that seeks more than the good of the society, is foundational in recognizing one's identity as a Christian. Throughout his writings, Augustine supports this view:

> It is we ourselves—we, His city—who are his best, his most glorious sacrifice. The mystic symbol for this sacrifice we celebrate our oblations familiar to the faithful.[48]

> "It follows that justice is found where God, the one supreme God, rules an obedient City according to his grace, forbidding sacrifice to any being save himself alone."[49]

---

45. Root, *Bonhoeffer as Youth Worker*, 50.
46. Root, *Bonhoeffer as Youth Worker*, 50.
47. Wilken, *The Spirit of Early Christian Thought*, 195.
48. Augustine, *City of God*, 10.7.
49. Augustine, *Exposition of Psalms*, 41.9.

"Where this justice does not exist, there is certainly no 'association of men united by a common sense of right and by a community of interests.' Therefore there is no commonwealth, for where there is no 'people,' there is no 'weal of the people.'"[50]

Wilken summarizes Augustine's view saying that "The greatest gift the church can give society is a glimpse, however fleeting, of another city, where the angels keep 'eternal festival' before the face of God."[51] Much in the way Augustine recognized a unique component to Christian identity, Bonhoeffer distinguishes the Christian community, not only in faith but in practice.

A Dialogical Community

Central to Bonhoeffer's approach was a sort of dialogical community which takes language seriously, intentionally engaging young people in thoughtful discussion. For instance, Ferdinand Schlingensiepen, in a biography on Bonhoeffer, notes that he wrote a catechism designed to "help create relational sharing through discussion."[52] Bonhoeffer, as well as many others, was beginning to criticize Luther's Shorter Catechism, which used a set of memorized questions and answers to drive home important biblical truths. Schlingensiepen explains Bonhoeffer's divergent approach saying, "They used the traditional format of questions and answers, but these were not to be learned by heart, becoming instead a stimulus for discussion with the young people."[53] Bonnhoeffer stresses a focus on concrete reality in ministering to young people, declining either an abstract application or a rote form of memory that bears no connection to reality. Instead he promotes genuine discussion around the application of one's faith.

It is interesting how Bonhoeffer's dialogical approach relates to Israel's mode of education. Israel's exchange of information between adult and child took on a very un-authoritarian and yet a very authoritative form.[54] Three characteristics can be identified which support this point: Teaching was open and easily dialogical (Deut 6:20–24), it was modeled on a sort of invitation to the child to ask questions, and the expected adult response

---

50. Augustine, *City of God*, 19.23.
51. Wilken, *The Spirit of Early Christian Thought*, 210.
52. Root, *Bonhoeffer as Youth Worker*, 92.
53. Schlingensiepen, *Dietrich Bonhoeffer 1906–1945*, 79–80.
54. Brueggemann, *The Creative Word*, 16.

included a form of testimonial evidence of their own faith.[55] This led to a natural conversation throughout one's development in which faith and the conversation around it became a sort of gift that was waiting for the opportune moment at which a young person was ready to engage.

The thrust of this ancient Jewish mode of education fits well with an idea that Bonhoeffer wrestles with throughout his entire ministry. This idea was apparent in Bonhoeffer's thinking from his first doctoral dissertation, *Sanctorum Communio*, all the way through to his prison letters. The idea is expressed in the German word *Stellvertretung*, best understood in English as "place-sharing," a level above the communal image of *Gemeinschaft*.

An example of this is found when Bonhoeffer finds himself appointed to a particularly unruly confirmation class in the Wedding district of Berlin[56] where he puts his theory into action: "Through stories Bonhoeffer invited the boys to share life together, to know him, so that they might in time give him the gift of knowing them, and in their mutual sharing of one to another, encounter the living Christ."[57] In entering into the boys' world in this way, Bonhoeffer displays an interest in them as people rather than as a project. His presence, as well as his composure throughout, communicated something deeper to them than any formal lesson he could have offered.[58]

It is not necessary to examine this particular instance deeply, but a summary of their response is telling:

> And with anxiety absent and the stories flowing, they felt ever drawn to him, willing to be led (the un-lead-able) and guided because each step they were assured he would take them to a place where their humanity would be affirmed and their person embraced in relationship. It was Bonhoeffer's composure and stories that became the buoyant waters that 'carried' the boys, allowing him to lead them.[59]

---

55. Brueggemann, *The Creative Word*, 16–18.

56. Root records the bedlam of this group of young boys: "The level of mayhem was so high that, in no exaggeration, these boys had killed their first teacher. Bonhoeffer was taking over because Johannes Maller simply could not handle the boys, leading him to great distress. A few weeks after handing the class over to Bonhoeffer, Pastor Maller had a heart attack and died. So it's not out of the question to suggest that Bonhoeffer was taking over a class that was so out of control that they had killed their last teacher." Root, *Bonhoeffer as Youth Worker*, 98.

57. Root, *Bonhoeffer as Youth Worker*, 99.

58. Root says, "His composure signaled to them that it might be that he is really just here for them, rather than to fulfill some goal that they could frustrate." Root, *Bonhoeffer as Youth Worker*, 100.

59. Root, *Bonhoeffer as Youth Worker*, 100.

In much the same way that Bonhoeffer sought to apply *Stellvertretung* to the young people to whom he ministered the theological campus seeks to build a community that makes genuine connection into the lived world of its students. To be purposeful in the time that students dedicate to vocational ministry formation, the theological campus must recognize the significance of such an approach. This mindset is well-proven in the age groups widely represented on college campuses today, Millennials and Generation Z. Chip Espinoza, Mike Ukleja, and Craig Rusch, in their book *Managing the Millennials: Discover the Core Competencies for Managing Today's Workforce*, identify a relational mindset for those who have been successful building partnerships with Millennials,[60] while Gen Z displays a much higher regard for relationship than for ideology.[61]

This kind of community is only made more important when one recognizes the emotional disconnect between young people and adults in Western culture today. Chap Clark recognizes a standard sense of adult abandonment among many young people as contemporary culture has moved from one that nurtures adolescents into adulthood to a devaluing of such a rite of passage.[62] Clark cites extensive research, along with his immersive study behind *Hurt 2.0*, to support this point of view. Clark notes that esteemed psychologist, Robert Epstein, contends that systems and structures erected to serve youth have actually held them back and even done them great damage, what he terms *infantilization*.[63] Clark also references David Elkind's argument that adults have failed in "enveloping" young people into set standards, values and beliefs in which "the adolescent can confront and challenge in order to construct and test out her own standards, values and beliefs."[64] The theological campus as an intentionally disengaged community fulfills this idea of enveloping students into a culture that ushers students along in their development. This type of community is vital in the process of re-forming the soul out of a culture that seems hellbent on deforming it from childhood.[65]

---

60. Espinoza et al., *Managing the Millennials*, 25–28.
61. *Gen Z*, 49–51.
62. Clark, *Hurt 2.0*, 7.
63. Clark, *Hurt 2.0*, 25–26.
64. Clark, *Hurt 2.0*, 26.
65. Palmer, "Toward A Spirituality of Higher Education," 75.

"Devoted" to Community

Kenda Creasy Dean took part in the NSYR as an interviewer and followed up with a look at those whom the study identified as the "devoted." The "devoted' were the 8% of young people interviewed who "attended religious services, weekly or more often, participated in religious youth groups, prayed and read the Bible regularly, and said they felt very close to God and that faith is extremely important in their lives."[66] By focusing directly on these young people, Dean has been able to map a way forward for those wishing to reclaim emerging generations for Christianity.

One of the definitive factors that Dean recognizes in these devoted young people is a cultural toolkit which enabled them to navigate their world. Ann Swidler, a sociologist, defines this cultural toolkit as "the symbols, stories, rituals, relationships, and worldviews that we pick up from our experience of the world around us—our default operating system—and we use them to construct meaning and guide our actions in the world."[67] Highly devoted young people in the NSYR demonstrated at least four of these characteristics: (1) confession to their tradition's creed; (2) belonging to a community that enacts the God-story; (3) a calling by this story to a larger purpose; (4) hope for the future promised by this story.[68]

Interestingly, the NSYR found the Mormon church to be exemplary in the rank of the devoted within adolescence, particularly in that Mormon teenagers were the most likely to hold similar religious beliefs to those of their parents.[69] The cause that Dean recognizes behind this is the homogeneity of their upbringing in the religious socialization of their Mormon communities.[70] Mormons plunge their young into a peculiar God-story

---

66. Dean, *Almost Christian*, 46.

67. As quoted in Dean, *Almost Christian*, 48.

68. Dean, *Almost Christian*, 49.

69. Smith, *Soul Searching*, 35. Dean also notes of Mormon youth that "91% reported 'few or no doubts' about religious beliefs in the past year." Dean, *Almost Christian*, 52–53.

70. Although Dean notes that this is not all positive: "Intense religious socialization and teaching in Mormon communities comes at a price. Mormon teenagers tend to be the 'spiritual athletes' of their generation, conditioning for an eternal goal with an intensity that requires sacrifice, discipline, and energy. Long before their classmates are smacking their snooze alarms, more than half of Mormon teenagers are rolling out of bed at 5:00 a.m., every single day for four years straight, in order to attend seminary. Seminary is frequently taught by a parent and typically involves reflexive practices like journaling about one's life and spiritual growth, as well as practical advice on how to plan and save for a two-year mission commitment to service and evangelism." Dean, *Almost Christian*, 50.

and surround them with articulate adults who demonstrate and support the Mormon worldview. In these communities, Mormons also encourage public discourse about faith at a higher percentage than any other faith surveyed by the NSYR;[71] however, the researchers' perception of these youth was that they were often more interested in giving the "correct" answer than that they were prepared to live these realities out beyond their communities.

In the Churches Engaging Young People (CEYP) project from 2012–15, the Fuller Youth Institute (FYI) sought to discover how churches were best engaging young people and retaining their commitment into their emerging adult years.[72] Although many of the characteristics of the Mormon community were evident, one trait in Christian churches effectively engaging young people was unique: "an accepting, authentic, and caring culture that fostered a sense of belonging . . . the FYI research team termed this frequently mentioned cluster of qualities 'warmth.'"[73] This cluster of qualities included descriptors such as welcoming, accepting, belonging, authentic, hospitable, and caring.[74] The CEYP study demonstrated a higher faith maturity and vibrancy in the emerging adults connected to these kind of communities,[75] as well as a deeper sense of community than simply meeting together or cooperating, but a sense of actually *becoming part of one another*.[76] The warmth of the community, then, determined the ability to be able to engage within as well as beyond the church walls.

Strategic Reengagement

It is imperative that a disengaged community, however, remember that its ultimate goal is the re-engagement of its members into the world-at-large.

71. "Faith communities that encourage public conversation about faith also help teenagers develop religious articulacy. Mormons (72%) and conservative Protestants (56%) are especially apt to share their religious beliefs with people not from their faith, compared to only 37% of Catholic youth." Dean, *Almost Christian*, 136.

72. The original published study and its findings can be found in Powell et al., *Growing Young*.

73. Powell et al., *Growing Young*, 166. In a follow up study—Greenway et al., "Getting Warmer."—FYI noted the importance of developing an assessment tool to measure such "warmth."

74. Powell et al., *Growing Young*, 166.

75. Powell et al., *Growing Young*, 173.

76. Powell et al., *Growing Young*, 176.

Matthew 28:18–20 is commonly referred to as the Great Commission and is seen by many as Jesus' creation of the mission of the church.[77] It is notable then that Jesus' language specifically tells his first followers to "go" and to preach the gospel to "all nations." Throughout Jesus' ministry one sees him inviting others to himself, but the instruction he leaves for the church is to "go."

The question, then, for the theological campus is how one best prepares a twenty-first-century emerging adult for such a task. It is evident from the preceding pages that these young people face a culture much different from the one that previous generations would recognize. Our next task, then, is to map the course for this kind of calculated reengagement.

Lovers of Truth

Os Guinness presents an image that is helpful in this examination. To begin, he notes the unique nature of this age and the practice of proclamation within it: "That . . . we are in the grand secular age of apologetics. The whole world has taken up apologetics without ever using or knowing the idea as Christians understand it."[78] Guinness sees in this secular age great potential for Christian evangelism,[79] however, he warns that this will look differently than in previous generations.

It is not necessary to fully unpack Guinness' slant here, but it is useful to examine a few aspects. Guinness claims that Christian proclamation is "a lover's defense"[80] and as such it should be deeper than what some have adapted as a cold, logical approach to apologetics. Although this emotion ought to be assumed in the life of the Christian, one's love of truth must also be evident. In making this argument, Guinness cites book 10 of Augustine's *Confessions*:

> Man's love of truth is such that when he loves something which is not the truth, he pretends to himself that what he loves is the truth, and because he hates to be proved wrong, he will not allow himself to be convinced that he is deceiving himself. So he hates the real truth for what he takes to his heart in its place.[81]

---

77. Wright, *Jesus and the Victory of God*, 297.
78. Guinness, *Fool's Talk*, 16.
79. Guinness, *Fool's Talk*, 16.
80. Guinness, *Fool's Talk*, 57.
81. Augustine, *Confessions* 10.23.

The Christian apologist has often been guilty of just such a sin, and it must be admitted that this has had at least some effect on the inherent suspicion of religious orthodoxy and authority in many of today's emerging adults.[82] This kind of approach could quickly fall victim to what Socrates called the "unexamined life" and what Martin Heidegger called "strategies for inauthenticity." Again, Guinness notes classical teaching that warns against such a stance, this time from Pascal:

> On this point, therefore, we condemn those who live without thought for the ultimate end of life, who let themselves be guided by their own inclinations and their own pleasures without reflection and without concern, and, as if they could annihilate eternity by turning away their thought from it, think only of making themselves happy for the moment.[83]

Pascal's warning to "those who live without thought for the ultimate end of life" certainly applies just as much to the Christian apologist who loses himself, or his gospel, in his argument. Guinness' approach then to Christian persuasion takes on a profoundly *unapologetic* stance:

> Apologetics may at times be brilliant, complex and scholarly, and climb to a rarified altitude at which only a few thinkers can breathe easily. It may therefore at times appear a long way from the simplicity of the gospel, but it must never be made into an end in itself, and it should never stand by itself. As the early church boasted rightly, the message of Jesus is both simple enough for a child to paddle in and deep enough for an elephant to swim in.[84]

A New Brand of Apologetics

Apologetics, alongside classes emphasizing personal evangelism, have traditionally been a strong focus of the theological campus in training ministers for the proclamation of the gospel. Cultural reengagement as presented here serves as a reminder that an emphasis on these practices remains important, but that the approach to each of these practices ought to be re-considered. The swing in cultural values moving into the twenty-first century—especially the move into post-Christendom and its close relation to postmodern

---

82. Bergler, *The Juvenilization of American Christianity*, 221.
83. Pascal, *Pensees*, p. 66.
84. Guinness, *Fool's Talk*, 111.

thought[85]—requires that the evangelist[86] take a different tack than in previous generations in Western history. Just as the NSYR demonstrated that young people raised in families emphasizing daily faith conversations were much more likely to retain their childhood faith,[87] twenty-first-century evangelism requires a sort of conversational Christianity that allows one's faith to be belief without the intrusion of scientific certainty.

James K. A. Smith sees this as a necessity, specifically that the Christian reject the need to "know" and instead remember that we are called to "believe." Smith says, "The best we can do is *believe*. Why? Because to know would mean being certain. We know that such certainty is an impossible dream; therefore, we actually lack knowledge. We don't know; we can only believe."[88]

Interestingly, one of Israel's great tasks in the education of its young was to build a yearning in which children longed to be part of just such a mysterious faith.[89] This longing was built through daily discussion as Israel walked out Deuteronomy 6:6–7: "And these words that I command you today shall be on your heart. You shall teach them diligently to your children, and shall talk of them while you sit in your house, and when you walk by the way, and when you lie down, and when you rise." This conversational faith not only solidified Jewish young people in their belief but prepared them to pass it along to the next generation. In much the same way this conversational approach lights the way in preparing theological students for effective re-engagement into the culture of the twenty-first century.

Immersive Language

In many ways the theological campus is an ideal environment for such preparation. Dean notes that such a language requires an integration

---

85. Although this paper has chosen in part to focus on secularism and its effects on today's emerging adults, both post-Christendom and postmodernism are in close relation in presenting similar challenges in raising up the next generation. For a good primer on post-Christendom and its effects, as well as a Christian response, see Murray, *Post-Christendom*. For another look at postmodernism and a Christian response, see Smith, *Who's Afraid of Postmoderism?*

86. "Evangelist" here is intended in its most basic definition as one who proclaims the gospel, not in the more precise use of "office" in which it is often used.

87. Dean, *Almost Christian*, 135–37.

88. Smith, *Who's Afraid of Postmodernism*, 118–19.

89. Brueggemann, *The Creative Word*, 16.

identified in situated learning theory as "legitimate peripheral participation," which "refers to the way newcomers become integrated into communities—namely, by participating in them."[90] Language, however, is key to this integration. Hauerwas likens this process to that of being an apprentice in the stone carver trade and that the initial task involved is to imitate the *speech*—not the skills—of the master by engaging in the art of eavesdropping. He says, "Note the order. Speech precedes practice, which precedes virtues . . . You adjust to being a stone carver by talking."[91] The NSYR demonstrates clearly the value of this model in the corollary religious devotion in adolescents;[92] however, this conversational approach also places a high emphasis on immersion into the process. The theological campus fits this description, being a locus for students' immersion into the Christian community and engaging them in the practice of applying one's argument to the cultural milieu.

Exilic Strategies for the Theological Campus

It is natural to see the exilic community in focus here, especially in its deliberate stance against the dominant culture, first in its intentional disengagement, and secondly through its preparation for reengagement. The question, though, is how the theological campus intentionally prepares students throughout this process for successful proclamation upon full reengagement with an unfriendly society. Brueggemann unpacks what he deems "Disciplines of Readiness" in concluding his metaphorical look at the contemporary church with that of the exile.[93] These disciplines "permit a rethinking of what exiles must do that usually is not done by preexilic people."[94] In these practices of new hope, one can see Kinnaman and Matlock's conclusion that the culture of today demands different preparation than did the culture of previous generations.[95]

---

90. Dean, *Almost Christian*, 145.

91. Hauerwas, "Carving Stone: Learning to Speak Christian."

92. "In the NSYR, three out of five youth named one or more adults in their congregations, other than their parents, to whom they can turn to for support, advice, and help. *In fact, the number of adults available for such support (in churches and elsewhere) rose proportionally to teenagers' religious devotion.*" Dean, *Almost Christian*, 152, emphasis added.

93. Brueggemann, *Cadences of Home*, 118–33.

94. Brueggemann, *Cadences of Home*, 118.

95. Kinnaman and Matlock, *Faith for Exiles*, 28.

Exiles in Training

Brueggemann begins by emphasizing the importance of the exilic community being "driven back to its most *dangerous memories*."[96] A community that is in danger of losing its identity to the dominant culture must maintain its distinction in this way. Israel was often tempted to succumb to a memory that was more culturally respectable and less radical,[97] likewise the church in secular culture must be careful it holds to its distinction even as culture pushes it more and more to the margins.[98]

Secondly, Brueggemann recognizes that exiles "must practice critical distance from their context, indeed, must practice *dangerous criticism* to keep visible the destructive seduction of the empire that is too often covered over by euphemism."[99] Interestingly, FYI's *Sticky Faith* study demonstrated the importance of parents in defining this critical distance for their adolescents, specifically avoiding easy answers.[100] As researchers have followed up on the initial study group, they have identified this "distance" as a continuing important trend, even into one's college years.[101] This distance—even critical distance—is imperative not only in maintaining one's faith but in being able to present its distinctives.

This speaks clearly to the third point Brueggemann makes, that in order to resist syncretism, "exiles are invited to practice *dangerous promises*."[102] Although it is important to maintain distance as noted above, that distance must be a purposeful distance. Specifically, Brueggemann's call brings to mind scriptures which present a dangerous worldview, passages that pastors often find too difficult to preach.[103] However, William Willimon, Pro-

---

96. Brueggemann, *Cadences of Home*, 118, emphasis original.

97. Brueggemann, *Cadences of Home*, 119–21.

98. James K. A. Smith speaks to this especially in engaging the postmodern culture: "Our understanding of what it means to be the church must be shaped by the priority of revelation and the Christian tradition, not what (even) a postmodern culture needs or is looking for. A radically orthodox church practice will refuse the correlational idol of relevance without giving up the central impetus of hospitality." Smith, *Who's Afraid of Postmodernism*, 126.

99. Brueggemann, *Cadences of Home*, 121.

100. Powell and Clark, *Sticky Faith*, 39–40.

101. Cheryl A. Crawford shared in a presentation at the 2018 Association of Youth Ministry Educators conference that one of the key indicators of a college person's ability to maintain their faith in college was their involvement and engagement in a campus Christian fellowship or ministry group within the first two weeks. Crawford and Gillooley, "Sticky Faith Turns 30."

102. Brueggemann, *Cadences of Home*, 124, emphasis original.

103. Willimon, "Postmodern Preaching" particularly notes the "thickness" of

fessor of the Practice of Christian Ministry and Director of the Doctor of Ministry program at Duke Divinity School, sees just these passages and the "thickness" of them as essential to the exilic existence. Willimon notes such texts as "seemingly disordered, often exasperating, sometimes threatening" which "have portrayed the true God truthfully."[104] Willimon even speaks to the apparent effect of these Scriptures in his own experience: "In fact, over time, many of us come to believe that these texts are true to the living God of Israel precisely because they are so seemingly disordered, exasperating, and threatening."[105] The language of faith must be one that is taught through the lens of these dangerous promises.[106]

As mentioned above, it seems the more culture has shifted away from God the less ministerial training has required an intentional disengagement from the anti-Christ culture. As the Apostle John recognized a similar condition in the first century, he called on the church to be anointed (χρῖσμα). This word draws on the image of oil or ointment being smeared on especially in the inaugural anointing ceremony for priests; also, often equated in NT contexts with the anointing of the Holy Spirit or the formal equation of the baptismal proclamation.[107] Being set apart in this manner indicates something more than mere separation, identifying the *radical* differences within one's Christian identity. A remembering and participation in dangerous promises calls on Christians to differentiate themselves and to learn a proclamation that more precisely scrutinizes these distinctions.

Fourth, Brueggemann notes that dangerous new songs must be sung,[108] specifically with an emphasis on poetic expression. He says that poetic language is "outrageous and unreasonable" and "invites exiles to sing against reality, to dance toward a future not even discernible" and "to

---

preaching of the prophetic texts and the heaviness of their message to societies that had likewise turned their backs on God.

104. Willimon, "Postmodern Preaching," 113.

105. Willimon, "Postmodern Preaching," 114.

106. Fuller Youth Institute's *Sticky Faith* study also demonstrated this. The authors of this study note how the lack of "dangerous" conversations have effected college students, especially those who have abandoned their faith, noted directly in a study by sociologist Derek Melleby from the Center for Parent/Youth Understanding: "In many cases, these teens reported having important questions regarding faith during adolescence . . . that were ignored by their parents or pastors rather than taken seriously and engaged thoughtfully." Powell and Clark, *Sticky Faith*, 91.

107. Bauer et al., *A Greek-English Lexicon of the New Testament and Other Early Christian Literature*, 894.

108. Brueggemann, *Cadences of Home*, 126.

praise the faithful God who will not be held captive by imperial reality."[109] Dean sees just this kind of language in the art of testimony: "Consequently, testimony tells the story of God in Jesus Christ using speech that is passionate, subjective, and invested. Testimony neither dissects an argument, nor makes one; it is more inclined to *sing*."[110] This is the difference between the learning of apologetics and the formation of intimate proclamation, which is unaware whether it is appropriate or inappropriate but spills out of the very essence of the passion of the one who believes.

Conclusion

The last two exilic merits recognized by Brueggemann are played out in various acts of worship. These are not as applicable here, but his overall point is essential to recognize in light of the exilic nature of twenty-first-century emerging adults in America: "This poetic alternative begins in recognizing our true situation; it moves by subversive, evangelical lips uttering hopes and possibilities; it may end in a new people, new community, new creation."[111] A people who wish to maintain their identity must go beyond memory and they must initiate an intense practice of hope. The exilic community must in essence learn to argue against the self-evident reality of their circumstances and cling to a hope that often seems unreal. This hope, then, is found in what Brueggemann describes as doxologies of defiance: "In the exile, the doxologies are not primarily acts of remembering God's past 'wonders' but anticipatory assertions concerning what God is about to do."[112] The exilic community must sing a new song, not one of memory, but one of faith for what is yet to come. Emerging adults today are more than ever a spiritual blank slate, with double the amount of Generation Z identifying as atheists as compared to adults and only 4 percent having a biblical worldview.[113]

The theological campus plays a central role in raising up generations who will not only maintain their faith in an unfriendly culture but will communicate it in a way that entices their peers to belief. The power of language in the exilic community cannot be overstated. For the theological

---

109. Brueggemann, *Cadences of Home*, 126.
110. Dean, *Almost Christian*, 148, emphasis added.
111. Brueggemann, *Cadences of Home*, 133.
112. Brueggemann, *Cadences of Home*, 20.
113. *Gen Z*, 27.

student to effectively engage their culture, it is imperative that their time on campus be intentionally rooted in purposeful disengagement, calculated reengagement, and that they are learning disciplines for readiness that will sustain their faith and position them to best proclaim the message in a way that engages the culture in which they live.

7

Interview Methodology

IT SHOULD BE NOTED that the interview portion of this study was not designed as a comprehensive examination of the material covered previously, nor should it be seen as anecdotal to the literature review. The intention in conducting interviews with emerging adults on a theological campus was to allow students to speak into this study and to give voice to their own experience of the above material.

An Explanation of the Study

It was my notion entering this project that measuring the use of language and one's ability to verbalize their faith would require a creative approach. For this study I decided that the best approach would be a phenomenological approach in the model of Irving Seidman. In this model, the interviewer is to consider four phenomenological themes:

1. The temporal and transitory nature of human experience
2. Whose understanding is it? Subjective understanding
3. Lived experience as the foundation of "phenomena"
4. The emphasis on meaning and meaning in context[1]

My job in this study was to insert myself into the experience of the students on the campus of TBCGS, to seek understanding in their lived

---

1. Seidman, *Interviewing as Qualitative Research*, 15–20.

experience and to hear how they have found meaning (growth) in their faith during their time on a theological campus.

As a way to gain access to student experience, I have incorporated a few methods to hear directly from them. These means were selected to accomplish a few important goals: (1) to establish a "live" conversation in which students could share freely, (2) to give me a baseline understanding for each individual student and where their level of comfort in proclaiming their faith began in their theological training and (3) to measure the influence of theological education on their ability to verbalize their faith.

Ministerial students on campus for leadership training the weeks leading up to the fall 2018 semester were presented with the opportunity to take part in a study entitled *Sacred Speech*. As I presented this opportunity, it was first important to explain why this study was necessary and how it would be informed by recent research. I presented a general overview of emerging adulthood and explained to the group why it was important to continue this research. Namely, I told the students this study was important to me, as a practical theologian, so that I might be able to gain a deeper understanding of a developmental stage that is stretching to the late twenties and, thus, a definitive factor for the church's future. The Vice President of Student Affairs had allowed some time for a presentation in the students' schedule, so I treated this as an opportunity to inform and to solicit participation.

As I considered how to conduct a study measuring students' growth in faith proclamation, I came to the conclusion that classic terms such as "witness" and "sharing one's faith" carried a negative connotation for many of our students, and that the perception of these were not in line with the proposal I have decided to put forth in this project. Attempting to circumvent the negative feelings that I had previously encountered in these kinds of discussions, I presented students with a different opportunity, instead simply asking them to *tell their story*. This served as an attempt to gauge their engagement with their own experiences while on campus and to ask them to measure their growth in being able to carry on faith conversations. These "God stories"[2] would set the stage for further reflection, as students

---

2. The term "God stories" will be used throughout the remainder of this study, referring specifically to these stories and also to a general understanding of encounters with God and how these experiences, alongside sound theology as presented on a theological campus, inform students' ability to proclaim their faith. In short, how do students see their story aligning with God's story and how do they learn to communicate this to others?

were challenged to reflect upon particularly formational moments during their time on campus and then to speak to how these moments influenced them in particular. From these experiences, students would reflect upon their growth in faith proclamation and how that had developed on campus, and whether this further enabled them to do so beyond the friendly theological campus environment.

This study approached emerging adulthood through Arnett's "self-focused" theory as compared to Christian Smith's "self-centered" view.[3] This meant that my goal throughout was not to identify specific issues as *problems* within emerging adulthood[4] but to approach this study through the lens of cultural influence and how best to respond to the lived experience of today's emerging adults.

Selecting the Study Group

In order to complete such a study, it was necessary to choose a sampling of students that reflected the theological campus and its mission accurately. This meant that the study group should reflect diversity in age, gender, and church background.[5] It was essential to limit this study to students with some level of experience on the campus and to students with a ministerial major.

A natural group to interview were the Resident Assistants, or RAs, who served as leaders in a multitude of ways throughout the life of the campus. These students represented a broad sample, including a balance of gender, year of study and field of study (see figures 2–4).

---

3. Arnett, *Emerging Adulthood*, 236–37; 242–43.

4. As in Smith, *Lost in Transition*.

5. It should be noted here that Trinity Bible College and Graduate School is located in the upper midwestern United States and thus does not have as racially diverse of a campus as in other parts of the country or the world. Although I have done my best to represent a level of diversity in other areas in these interviews, it must be conceded that the sample group falls short in racial diversity.

FIGURE 2: R.A. GENDER

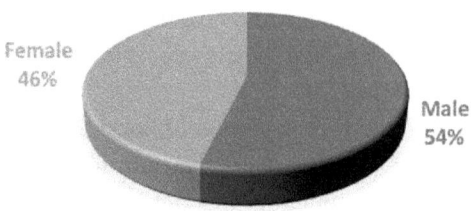

FIGURE 3: R.A. YEAR OF STUDY

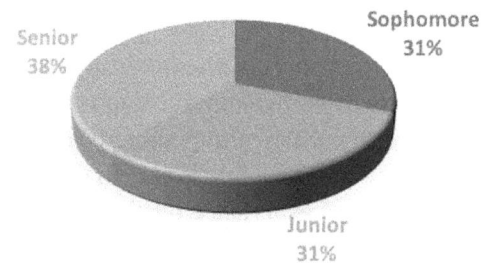

FIGURE 4: R.A. FIELD OF STUDY

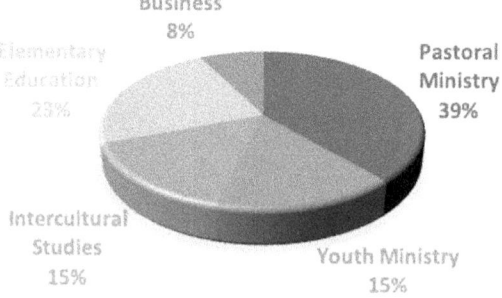

Initially this study was presented to the Resident Assistants across all fields of study, however, in time it became clear that the most appropriate candidates were those pursuing some sort of vocational ministry degree. This narrowed the original study group from a potential of thirteen

Interview Methodology

students down to ten, eliminating only one sophomore and two seniors, and maintained a level of diversity in gender, year of study and field of study (see figures 5–7).

FIGURE 5: STUDY GROUP GENDER

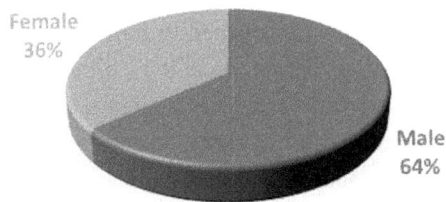

FIGURE 6: STUDY GROUP YEAR OF STUDY

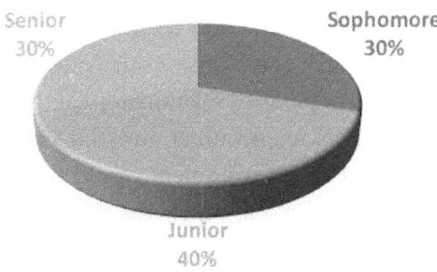

FIGURE 7: STUDY GROUP FIELD OF STUDY

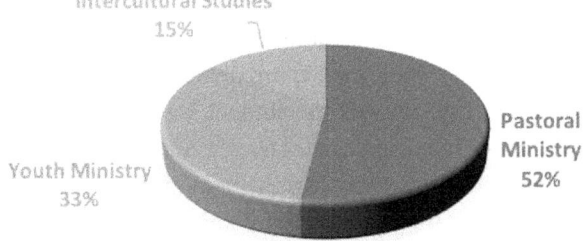

An Explanation of the Interviews

In the initial presentation of the *Sacred Speech* study, I presented an overview of the National Study of Youth and Religion (NSYR), specifically focusing in on the *de facto* religious beliefs identified and categorized as Moralistic Therapeutic Deism. Specifically, I highlighted the effect which identified that otherwise articulate young people "stammered and groped for words when the conversation turned to religion, as if no one had ever asked them these questions before, or as if . . . in another language."[6] The students were presented with language as the central component of this study and that an examination of their "stories" while at TBCGS would help to inform the influence of the theological campus on the formation of "Christian language" or faith proclamation.[7]

The First Set of Interviews

For each of the following interviews, I engaged students in a warm, hospitable room filled with couches and used most regularly for daily coffee times among the staff. The president of our college commonly describes this gathering room as a place of relational breakthrough for our school, and so I felt it appropriate to encounter our students' "God stories" in this location. I also felt that the environment would invite hospitality both in sharing and receiving and would open the door to a deeper communal sense, rather than that of a detached academic study. I wanted these interviews to feel less like an exam and more like a conversation over coffee. For this approach I must also thank my wife, who prepared fresh baked goods for each of the interviews. These, along with fresh brewed coffee and the living room feel of the room, provided a welcome environment that encouraged openness in our conversation.

The first study group took part approximately three weeks into the fall semester of 2018. This allowed the student leaders to attend to their responsibilities in the first few weeks of classes. Prior to the first interviews, students were given two weeks to put together a catalog of four to seven pictures from across campus that represented "God stories" during their time on campus. These "God stories" were defined as "moments of encounter

---

6. Dean, *Almost Christian*, 15–16.

7. The term "Christian language" is used interchangeably with the concept of faith proclamation throughout the study.

with God which changed their outlook and affected their trajectory forward." This definition was intentionally vague in an attempt to examine the student's self-understanding of such a moment. Their understanding of a "God story" could immediately provide a baseline in their ability to speak of their faith.

The organization of these pictures was also left intentionally vague prior to the interview, although students were invited to place their stories into chronological order as they presented them to the group. By asking students to formulate their stories chronologically, it opened the door to identify if there was a progressive nature to these experiences and that in itself would help to identify students' growth.

Each student responded with at least four pictures, giving an explanation and fitting the moment into their overall story of faith development on campus. I decided to conduct these interviews in a large group format, hoping to spark further engagement between students and to further elucidate their understanding of their experience. Students were also asked to note important people or events in these experiences and what specifically was different in their current state as a result of these experiences. For the purposes of this study, the experiences themselves were not at the forefront, but the students' ability to articulate what had happened and the influence on their faith.

The Second Set of Interviews

The second study group was broken up into three smaller groups, specifically seeking to create a more intimate environment and to encourage interaction. The first interviews were conducted one at a time in a group setting, but these were presented as an open discussion, inviting students to contribute at any time encouraging interaction between students. As the first interviews were designed to examine students' ability to verbalize their "God stories," the second interviews were designed to note their level of confidence and engagement among their campus peers and beyond.

Prior to the second interviews, students were asked to take note of their interactions with others on campus for approximately one month before coming together to review these instances. *How did they use their "God stories" to speak into the lives of others?* These stories moved students from telling of their own formation to examples of how they had learned to engage others through their growth and experience.

To open these interviews, students were asked to recall an instance in which they used their "God stories" to engage with other students. For example, as they interacted with freshman, did they find themselves referring back to stories shared in the first interviews of their own early college experiences? If they did, they were asked to explain how they found themselves using these stories.

The goal of this approach was not to gauge the effectiveness of the students' leadership or even to measure the value of each individual statement. The objective was to note the use of their experiences and how this informed their faith articulation. Did their experience and their stories speak to a deeper faith language that had taken root through their theological education? Did their language reflect that of mature Christian faith or that of the Moralistic Therapeutic Deism so prevalent in the twenty-first-century church? Although this study was based on the overall campus experience, I also pursued the integration of students' classroom experience into this discussion.[8]

Once all students had the opportunity to share their campus experiences, I turned the question to address their engagement off campus. As much as their engagement on campus played a role in this study, their engagement outside of the friendly confines of the campus would be perhaps even more telling.

At the end of these interviews I presented a brief survey, asking students to rate their confidence in verbalizing their faith on a scale of one through ten. They were first asked to answer this question regarding their first day on campus (presumably as a freshman) and then to answer in the present tense. This survey was an attempt to measure the student's increase in confidence, and if in fact this was evident to them.

As noted above, one of the key findings of the NSYR was a lack of confidence in what one believed, thus leading to an inability to articulate beliefs. On the flip side, devoted young people easily discussed faith matters and demonstrated a natural ability in such discussions.[9] As such, it seemed a measure of the students' growth in confidence would go a long

---

8. For instance, I might ask a student to explain where they learned a particular theological concept that they had mentioned. In many cases, the students could point to a specific class or discussion with a professor where they came to a better understanding of their faith. In some cases, this understanding proved enough to give them the ability to apply it in proclamation, whereas in others the campus emphasis on experiential learning was noted.

9. Dean, *Almost Christian*, 40–42.

Interview Methodology

way towards understanding whether or not the campus was accomplishing the goal of instilling a "Christian language" or not.

As one who interacts with his study group on a day-to-day basis, I have done my best to limit the scope of this study to the formal interviews discussed above. However, if it seemed that a peripheral conversation would prove pertinent to the findings of the study, this has been included with an explanation of its origins.

8

In Their Own Words

AT THE OUTSET OF this analysis, it is imperative to remind the reader that the intention behind these interviews was to provide a sample of emerging adults the opportunity to speak for themselves on the topics examined at length previously in this study. Although they were not aware of the findings presented up to this, I felt it necessary to hear from students in order to set their experiences alongside the research we have already examined. It is also important to recall that although the inability to verbalize faith is indicated throughout the NSYR,[1] the follow-up studies examining emerging adulthood do not address this in detail.[2] A more sizeable study group would be necessary to provide empirical evidence as to the consistency of this characteristic with the adolescents of the NSYR; however, this would also run the risk of losing the intended intimacy with the interviews. The strength of this study, in my opinion, is the familiarity with the students and their willingness to openly share from their experience. This study, then, serves in contributing to a broad conversation on the topic of reclaiming the "Christian language" among emerging adults.

As the outset, several questions came to the forefront: How apparent was the impact of secularism and the privatization of faith in the lives of these students? How were they both similar and different from the

---

1. Specifically, in Smith, *Soul Searching*, and Dean, *Almost Christian*.

2. Although this language piece is predominantly covered in the initial findings of the NSYR, follow-up contributions have lacked a precise look at this issue. See Smith, *Souls in Transition*, Smith, *Lost in Transition*, and Arnett, *Emerging Adulthood*, in which his religious perspective is based largely off of the results of the NSYR.

emerging adults highlighted in the follow up interviews to the NSYR? If there were differences, what role had the theological campus played in this distinction? And lastly, could the exilic metaphor of the church be a useful lens through which to understand the role of the theological campus?

Although this chapter will seek to compare the emerging adults in this study with the statistical data of the NSYR and its follow-up research, a disclaimer is in order. The limitation of this project requires that one particular group of students has been observed (TBCGS students with a vocational ministry emphasis), while the control group is provided through the data of the existing research which has already been covered. I also must admit that one of these groups holds personal value for me, while the other is represented mostly in the data.

Evidentiary Influence of Secularism

The first question was whether students demonstrated characteristics of those affected by the secular culture, marginalized in their faith proclamation. As noted at length above, many of these students have grown up in a world where faith has been given little objective value and such a language is deemed useful only in religious settings. Did these students, each of them preparing for some sort of vocational ministry, demonstrate traits of a culture that devalues the public proclamation of one's faith? This would determine whether the hypothesis, as demonstrated particularly in the NSYR, was indeed apparent in this group of emerging adults.

The study group was made up of emerging adults from different backgrounds, to some degree already described above. More in particular, though, some grew up in church, while others only came to faith in their last years of high school. Some have radical stories of faith—bouts with suicide, extreme struggles with identity and belonging, and so on—while others come from seemingly model backgrounds. In short, even as these students represented a sort of elite selection from a theological campus, they displayed characteristics reminiscent of the familiar struggles of the average emerging adult. In fact, the interviews seemed to prove that these students, at least in part, demonstrated the same effects of secularism as are recognized across the culture.

First of all, this was evident in the way that almost all of these students recognized the theological campus as a place of belonging for those with faith; perhaps even the first such place many of them had ever experienced.

Particularly, students said that they found the theological campus to be one of the first places in which they ever encountered adults who provided an authentic and thoughtful example of faith. One student spoke of coming to freshman orientation and feeling as though they were "home" in that moment, while another described their campus experience as the first time he understood what it meant to be a part of the Body of Christ. Again, the terminology of "home" was prominent, as this student explained that they had never felt "at home" in their faith prior to their time on campus.[3]

Basic developmental factors are clearly evident in these statements, as college students begin to take ownership of their identity in these (self-focused) years. However, the emphasis on faith seems to indicate that many had not previously felt welcome in expressing their faith. The theological campus provided something that their churches and other communities were unable to deliver throughout their childhood: an all-encompassing environment that allows an integration of faith into all facets of life.[4]

In fact, this "all-encompassing environment" was often evident in the students' emphasis on Christian community, beyond relational traits,

---

3. It should also be noted that "home" and "family" are terms often used to describe our small Bible college. As our VP of Student Development says in an opening letter of the Student Handbook, "Welcome to the Trinity family! We are glad you have chosen to be a part of this community. Our College is a unique place. We are small enough to know your name but big enough to believe in your dreams! The Trinity family is committed to journey with you as you discover the calling on your life—and then educate, empower, and position you to fulfill that call." https://www.trinitybiblecollege.edu/docs/pdfs/20-21-student-handbook.pdf.

4. Prior to accepting a faculty position at TBCGS, I was considering a position as a Bible teacher in a Christian high school. This school, along with others in the region, were employing a curricular approach called "Teaching for Transformation." This curriculum is designed as a holistic approach to education, in the form of Abraham Kuyper's famous quote: "There is not a square inch in the whole domain of human existence over which Christ, who is sovereign over all, does not cry, 'Mine!'" This curriculum employs "Core Practices" which employ "learning experiences that help students discover God's story and His fingerprints in all things, with the hope that every learning experience will become truly transformational for every student." I make no attempt to examine this approach in a higher educational context here (although there are correlations to the Integration Model discussed previously), but do note that some students in my study, although coming out of a Christian educational background with this intent in mind, continued to demonstrate the common factor of not being strong in their faith proclamation. With limited exposure to this theory in the back of my mind, I felt strongly that the reengagement piece of the exilic model would need to be emphasized and examined in this study. A more complete overview of the Teaching for Transformation approach to Christian secondary education can be found at https://cace.org/wp-content/uploads/2017/10/SCCS-TfT-Overview.pdf.

through the intentionality of a theological community.⁵ Almost all of these students expressed a satisfaction at being a part of a designated Christian community emerging from a culture that demonstrated little appreciation for their faith.

One student described this experience in an interesting manner. Being a good student and a high achiever throughout high school, she entered college with a similar mindset. It did not help that she also followed a sister who had graduated from the same college as valedictorian previously, which caused her to feel pressure to live up to the same standard. As she developed friendships on campus, however, the young woman described conversations that, "pushed me to think about things I didn't even want to think about." When asked to elaborate on this statement, she clarified that she had learned the value of questions versus the value of having the answers. In essence, this young woman found herself moving from a world in which her academic experience had been built upon finding answers, only to find herself in theological community that recognized education as a formational process of personhood.⁶

Secondly, students demonstrated their growth into a faith community and away from a worldview which marginalized their faith and its place in public discourse. Several students described early experiences at college and how they had grown to recognize spiritual truths, as though seeing these experiences through new eyes. In most of the students, there was a sequential nature to their "God stories," indicating that students had grown in the integration of their faith into the whole of their lives. These students had not only matured in their faith understanding, but also in

---

5. The identification of any given Christian community might take on many forms, including exilic (as has been addressed in this project), monastic, or ecclesial. The emphasis of students here was not focused toward any type of Christian communal system, but rather the intentionality of creating a communal environment. The purpose for addressing the exilic community in this project was specifically to attempt to offset students from a foreign culture and to examine the role of a theological campus in maintaining the Christian identity, specifically the faith language, in light of a culture of faith marginalization.

6. This general contrast in educational approach can be seen in W. H. Cowly's summation of America's transition to the research university in the latter part of the nineteenth century: "The old college had been an Alma Mater—albeit chiefly concerned with the religious welfare of students—but within its lights it saw the student as a whole person and not just a mind to be loaded with facts like a car tank with oil. German-trained professors, however, abandoned the holistic conception of the student and of education. In brief, they gave their allegiance to German-inspired impersonalistic intellectualism." Glanzer, "Who Are We to Form Students?," 111.

their ability to articulate these experiences. In short, students had come to a more poised connection between their story and God's story.

The way students communicated this was by describing a newfound "confidence" in the proclamation of their faith. Several students explained that their confidence had developed specifically through what they were learning in the classroom. One student described himself as one who "did not fully embrace what it meant to be Christian" before his time on campus. His newfound understanding of his faith led to a deeper confidence in how he could articulate his faith. Another young man, who was new to the faith when he entered college, described early experiences where he felt "behind others" in basic scriptural knowledge. It was his education, however, that had given him confidence to share what he had learned, even if he still recognized the need to grow.

Newfound educational acumen, however, was not the central component on the mind of most of the students. In fact, one student described a particular "God story" where a professor continued to care for her even when she did not perform up to her usual academic standard. She said, "They loved me when I was not impressive," noting that this made her feel as though she was "a peer and not a subordinate." This student summarized what seemed to be evident throughout the group: that they had experienced a noticeable shift from that of a detached student *performing* to make the grade, to instead a mentality more closely resembling that of a *partner* in their educational process. Many of these statements did not directly connect to faith proclamation, but students recognized a new authority in their language through experiences that gave them ownership of their mind and their personhood.

One student described that he had become much more willing to share with others what God had done in his life because of what he deemed the "communal invitation to the struggle." It was as if this invitation to authentic community had lifted the burden of perfection from his shoulders and he could now share what God was truly doing in his life. This confidence appears to have been impeded previously by contemporary culture, but students encountered freedom in a community in which he could authentically engage culture through a Christian worldview.

At the core of the above statements is the issue of *agency*. Psychologists, Richard M. Ryan and Edward L. Deci recognize agency in humanity as normative rather than exceptional and see the fullest form of humanity as "curious, vital, and self-motivated . . . agentic and inspired, striving to learn;

extend themselves; master new skills; and apply their talents responsibly."[7] The key is to allow this to happen in freedom, recognizing that all people are influenced by both extrinsic and intrinsic motivators; it is those who establish healthy self-regulation of these motivators who develop the most agency over their life.[8] That being said, they note that this level of agency can often be diminished through the influence of various socio-cultural influences. In the interviews that I conducted this depletion was evident, a reminder of the importance of identifying the ideal atmosphere to offset these effects on a theological campus.

Ryan and Deci concluded that conditions of "supportive autonomy and competence" facilitate agency, while those that "controlled behavior and hindered perceived effectance" encumber its expression.[9] This means that students pursuing theological education need campus communities that demonstrate a growth expectation alongside of a supportive atmosphere.

This became evident in my interviews, as several students demonstrated the influence of community alongside of a level of independence from the predominant religious worldview of their peers. One student came to college after having spent his life on the mission field in India. He described a predictable level of culture shock and the difficulty of initially feeling as though he had to "fake" being an American. He questioned the wisdom of coming to be educated in a place where he could not even understand the people. However, it was out of this experience that he learned to think

---

7. Ryan and Deci, "Self-Determination Theory" 68–78.

8. This is particularly helpful when it is set against the NSYR's examination of Mormon youth and the prior discussion regarding researcher's suspicions that such youth were giving answers they recognized as appropriate, and perhaps not being completely forthright in their responses. This, however, is not limited to other faith expressions. Consider the student studying on a satellite campus in a church setting. As they study in an environment that is most likely highly homogenous, both in theology and in practice, they are less likely to encounter difference from what they have previously known (especially if they attended this church previously). On a theological campus, students are forced to wrestle with subtle and not-so-subtle differences among their peers, as well as faculty and staff relationships, even on a campus that is united under a common theological tradition. In my view, this is not only positive if handled correctly, but it is necessary in our current cultural climate. This reality forces students to a deeper level of study and self-determination, which prepares them to proclaim their faith with a higher level of confidence in an unfriendly culture. They have not learned a brand of theology and ministry practice that works in a particular context but have been pushed to develop theological thought that prepares them for a much broader context.

9. Ryan and Deci, "Self-Determination Theory."

outside of himself, to be a giving and open person, rather than what he described as self-centered.

This language indicated an agency that runs counter to the kind of "therapeutic" language that was prevalent throughout the NSYR and its follow up studies. In fact, throughout the interviews I found little evidence of the therapeutic language of Moralistic Therapeutic Deism. Specifically, several students described the impact of two ministry immersion programs instituted at TBCGS over the last 6 years: a gateway-to-college program called Pack Your Bags[10] and annual "GO Trips."[11] These trips are a part of the intentional focus on experiential learning at TBCGS, which challenge students to apply what they are learning across a multitude of cultural ministry opportunities.

In describing these opportunities students noted moments that pushed them beyond their comfort zones where they learned to trust God in difficult situations. One student recalled the vivid experience of ministering on the Pine Ridge Native American Reservation in North Dakota. On this trip the student recalls realizing, maybe for the first time, that there was "more out there than me." Another student describes a trip to Spain and how the training for the trip gave her a new perspective on the gospel. This was "when the fullness of the gospel was revealed to me," she recalls.

These examples demonstrate that something unique happens when the campus looks for opportunities for students to *struggle* in their faith; *even to struggle in the proclamation of their faith*. It is not that students do not display the influence of culture, but that something special happens as they are challenged to function in a community that opens the door to confident Christian identity and empowers agency with which to proclaim God's gospel message.

---

10. A brief program description taken from http://www.packyourbagstbc.org: "*Pack Your Bags* (PYB) is designed for high school graduates looking to dedicate one year to seek God and serve others. It is particularly beneficial for those who are unclear about the next step in their lives. PYB positions students to hear God's voice through seeking, learning, and serving."

11. These "GO Trips" have included mission and service trips to international locations such as China, Spain, Australia, Japan, and the Dominican Republic, as well as domestic opportunities in both urban and rural settings.

In Their Own Words

Faithful Integration

In order to recognize the impact of the theological campus, a discussion from my second set of interviews will be helpful. In this conversation I asked students to share their experiences in sharing their "God stories" with others on campus. A young man described a certain "brother/sister" activity[12] where his students and a female RA's had come together for a Bible study.[13] It was during this discussion that the two RAs found a common supposition, even though their experiences could not have been more different.

The female student describes her background as an almost idyllic home life, with parents who regularly attend church and demonstrate their faith openly. The young man grew up in foster care, "surviving" a system which he admits has had an effect. Almost opposite backgrounds, and yet both had struggled in their identity, even if for different reasons. The young man had often felt the need to live as an unauthentic version of himself to feel accepted in different foster homes, while the young woman had learned to find her identity in *what she did* for Jesus and not *who she was* in him.

As the two described the interaction from this Bible study, they explained their surprise that such opposite experiences could lead to similar challenges. Both articulated a comfort in realizing that another could relate, but each also walked away with a new confidence in their faith language. The young man said that he grew in confidence in being able to speak into the life of *anyone*. He said, "Growing up in the lifestyle that I did you just assume people won't understand. And to find out that somebody who grew up in a very different lifestyle understands on a level that I couldn't comprehend was very eye opening, and also kind of reassuring to know that people from any walk can have the same kind of struggles and *you can speak into that*." The young woman recognized her ability to relate her story to another, after feeling previously that her story was less valuable than others. She said, "A lot of times coming from a church background you feel

---

12. At certain times throughout the school year, male and female dorms at TBCGS plan joint activities such as game nights, movies, off-campus activities, etc. that are called "brother/sister" evenings. As described on the TBCGS website Brother / Sister Floor Fellowships are "A time for Kesler, Liechty, and Riffe halls to break up and spend time with their assigned brother/sister floor. A great time of fellowship. These happen once a month throughout each semester." https://www.trinitybiblecollege.edu/atmosphere/campus-life.

13. A unique characteristic of a theological campus that cannot be ignored: that a "great time for fellowship" ends up being a Bible study!

like, 'I've lived this perfect life and I just really can't relate to people who have been in a really broken situation and stuff and they're not even going to want to receive this from me'... But realizing that we still have things in common and things that we can speak to each other, it was really cool for me to realize that even with other people you can still find the similarities and speak into that."

This discussion represents an example of the kind of interaction highlighted time and again by students in this study. The theological college campus offers a unique opportunity for students to encounter others and to wrestle with an integration of their faith alongside their lived experience. This study demonstrates a desire in students for this kind of integrative learning environment.[14]

Students' relationship with faculty was important in this discussion. Half of the students in the study mentioned faculty directly, while others alluded to them as they highlighted their integration of faith with everyday life through their stories. One student's first significant memory on campus was when a professor prayed for him during a chapel service. He expressed shock, saying the professor "prayed for me before I even knew who he was." Another student expressed surprise in his early experience that a professor took time to listen to him and to speak into his life. This relationship, he says, has since been replicated numerous times with different members of the faculty. One student summed up the impact of these statements when she said that these relationships have caused her to reflect upon her relationship with God, teaching her who God is in one's life. Several others in the room nodded their agreement with this statement. These relationships were not only academically formational for students, but they represented a deeper understanding, and indeed experience, of their relationship with God.

As students mentioned faculty in these conversations, they were quick to make the connection to the *person* beyond the role of the

---

14. In fact, the theological campus might stand apart from other higher education atmosphere's in this regard. Regarding the common experience, Barna's *Gen Z* study cited Alan Levinovitz in a defining mark of this generation to seek "safe spaces": "There a very real danger that these efforts [to institute trigger warnings and safe spaces] will become overzealous and render opposing opinions taboo. Instead of dialogues in which everyone is fairly represented, campus conversations about race, gender, and religion will devolve into monologues about the virtues of tolerance and diversity. Even though academic debate takes place in a community, it is also combat. Combat can hurt. It is literally offensive. Without offense there is no antagonistic dialogue, no competitive marketplace, and no chance to change your mind." The students in my interview, although a small sample, seemed quite averse against this thinking. *Gen Z*, 27.

professor. The personal interaction of faculty and willingness to continue conversations beyond the classroom led students to feel further valued as a person. They spoke clearly that they see these faculty "living out" their faith and that they are models for students across the campus. This speaks highly of faculty at TBCGS, which should be noted, but perhaps more importantly these statements speak to students' expectations of their professors beyond the classroom.

Again, throughout the interviews, students spoke of the importance of the palpable example of the faculty, not only as teachers but as mentors. In fact, this desire for mentors led to an interesting exchange as one student took exception to the premise of my study. As the student was presented with his ability to verbalize his faith off campus, he re-visited the statement from the NSYR on which this study is based. Suddenly he voiced a level of indignation at the idea that emerging adults today do not demonstrate the ability to verbalize their faith:

> I don't think the other generations should be saying that because I look back and I'm like "*I haven't seen other people from other generations verbalizing their faith.*" It's not an "our generation" problem, it's a multi-generational problem . . . *And if you want us to verbalize our faith better, then you better as an older generation represent verbalizing your faith too. Because we're not going to learn unless we have examples of generations above us.*

This poignant statement is a reminder that emerging adults are looking to adults to lead by example as students grapple with what it means to be Christian in today's world. The enthusiastic agreement expressed by the rest of the study group only confirms that this student said something that resonated with all of the others.[15]

---

15. Although this paper has emphasized the challenge of secularism, these interviews made clear a larger scope of concern. As these emerging adults prepare to enter ministry in a post-Christian, postmodern, among other "posts", young ministers-to-be seek examples of what it is to minister in a confounding world, and theological faculty play an important role in this. Stuart Murray describes this confounding transitional age in his work on post-Christendom: "Post-Christendom does not comprehensively describe the cultural shifts impacting Western societies. It is one of many 'post-' words signaling an experience of cultural turbulence, of transition from the known to the unknown. Familiar examples include 'post-modern,' 'post-industrial,' 'post-colonial,' 'post-secular,' 'post-structural,' and (the 'word of 2016,' according to the *Oxford English Dictionary*) 'post-truth.' The prefix means 'after' and indicates something familiar is passing. It says nothing about what is replacing it. We know things are not how they used to be and sense change in the air, but we are unsure what is approaching. 'Post-' words are backward

Emerging Voices

Are We Then Exiles?

The exilic model presented above seems a potentially helpful lens through which to see the theological campus and its mission in contemporary culture. As said at the outset of this chapter, though, it was my hope that these interviews could give emerging adults a voice in this process, not least in setting forward this proposition. Although there are many useful components of this model observable in the interviews, it is my view that this metaphor should only be applied within limits. Below I will attempt to briefly define these boundaries.

A Strange Optimism

First of all, it is important to note that none of these students would most likely describe themselves as exiles. Even as I broached the subject with a few of them outside of our formal interview sessions, their responses ranged from surprise to skepticism.[16] This in itself, however, is a matter of interest. Michael Frost, an Australian theologian, reflected upon Brueggemann's work on exile and described the contemporary church as "grieving its loss and . . . struggling with humiliation." In the same thought he calls the church to drastic action: "to express resentful sadness about what was, and now is not, and never will be again."[17] Frost's overall message here is not one of grief, but a hope that the end of Christianity's reign will bring a renewed sense of purpose and mission.

Students in the *Sacred Speech* study demonstrated a decidedly hopeful mindset, although their experience was slightly different than what Frost describes. For them this optimism was not based on a sense of loss or humiliation, but rather on the perception that the current age appears as everyday reality—almost mundane—for many of them, and the Christian

---

facing, indicating that something is disappearing. If we could describe the new reality raking shape, we would not use 'post-' language but would name it. Used in this way, this terminology displays humility: we do not have a full and accurate understanding of what is happening, but we know previous assumptions, structures, and responses are now inadequate. Christendom is dying: we are entering a new culture that is 'after Christendom' and we realize that we will need time to find our bearings in this new landscape." Murray, *Post-Christendom*, 4.

16. One student's response was especially telling: "Oh, that's the angle you are taking? Ok then."

17. Frost, *Exiles*, 9.

community of the theological campus presents a new *hope-filled* experience. Much of the student's optimism was in fact tied to this newfound reality of the Christian community, which had given them a missional outlook on their cultural engagement. Students discussed what they had learned from the campus community and how their *hope* was to replicate such an atmosphere in their future ministerial vocation.

If contemporary emerging adults do not see themselves well-suited within this exilic framework, however, we should ask whether this is a helpful lens through which to view them. Taylor believes that people tend to be narrative animals. He says, "we define who we are, and what we ought to do, on the basis of what story we see ourselves in."[18] At its core, this narrative is found in one's worldview, which James W. Sire compares to layers of one's consciousness in a recent book on worldview entitled *Naming the Elephant*. Once one drills in on the highest layer, Sire says, one finds "the highest order of our practical behavior—a comprehensive plan of life, a highest good, the highest norms of action, an ideal of shaping one's personal life as well as that of society."[19] How useful can this "exilic narrative" be if emerging adults do not themselves recognize the connection?

The answer seems to lie less in recategorizing students' self-identity and more in recognizing the changing role of the theological campus in the twenty-first century. Failure in making this distinction risks the danger of returning theological campuses to the separatist fundamentalism found in many of their mid-twentieth century origins,[20] a movement that retreated from culture in such a way that it denigrated the kind of integrative discussion highlighted throughout this project.[21] This approach ignores the

---

18. As quoted in Smith, *How (Not) to Be Secular*, 25. Charles Taylor also addresses this in Taylor, *A Secular Age*, 28: "Our understanding of ourselves and where we stand is partly defined by our sense of having come to where we are, of having overcome a previous condition."

19. Sire, *Naming the Elephant*, 25.

20. Joel A. Carpenter identifies the historical danger of such a mindset: "Many of today's evangelical colleges and universities were founded as Bible schools, whose first task may have been to train evangelists and missionaries, but later began to provide spiritual inoculations for those headed to the jungles of godless higher education." Carpenter, "The Mission of Christian Scholarship in the New Millennium," 71.

21. Barna's *Gen Z* study notes such a danger in the emerging generations and their lack of integrative discussion: "Many teens are deeply reluctant to make declarative statements about anything that could cause offense, and thus they struggle with anxiety and indecision when it's time to give an answer, or time to act on it." *Gen Z*, 28.

importance of reengagement that we have already discussed, and does little to build healthy engagement between theology and contemporary life.

In my opinion, the best application of the exilic lens is in building a framework for the theological campus to approach the contemporary world in conversation. As the Lutheran scholar Martin Marty says, "Conversation partners do not [claim to] know everything . . . They relish the presence of others, of those who are different; they enjoy the contributions of many."[22] As we have already discussed, this is a call to a new kind of apologetics; a return to *belief* from the land of *knowing*.

One student recognized this idea in her use of story as a tool in proclaiming her faith. She said, "I think we nowadays definitely use our story as maybe an entryway to like a connection point to God and yeah, I guess other generations might see that as different that we're just talking about ourselves, but I see it as like it starts with me." An "entryway" or "connection point" seems to be language befitting the kind of conversation Marty suggests. The question becomes: How does the theological campus foster such an environment? Ernest Boyer says:

> We urgently need to shape a curriculum that shows relationships, not fragmentation. Today's students are offered a grab-bag of isolated courses. They complete the required credits, but what they fail to gain is a more coherent view of knowledge and a more integrated, more authentic view of life. To put it simply, their sense of the sacred is diminished.[23]

This demonstrates the importance of the "disengaged" aspect of the exilic community: that the theological campus would intentionally set itself apart from the contemporary culture, although not necessarily against it. Perhaps, though, one of the weaknesses of the contemporary application is that the exilic view has been applied as a normative reality for the Christian community moving forward.[24] The biblical image of exile, however,

---

22. Jacobsen and Jacobsen, *Scholarship & Faith*, 47.
23. Jacobsen and Jacobsen, *Scholarship & Faith*, 50.
24. Especially that of Frost who seems to see exile as a continuing reality for the church. Frost does discuss an end to this exilic state in his epilogue, saying that John the Baptist's baptism "was a call for the Jews to prepare themselves spiritually for their exile to end;" however, he speaks throughout the book and in conclusion as though exile is an ongoing state of being. Frost's metaphor, then, seems to be a normative reality for all Christians into eternity when "those who yearn for home will see that their exile from God ends right now in Christ." Frost, *Exiles*, 326–27.

is never intended as a new normal but is a peculiar and temporary state in which the people of God find themselves.[25]

This underlines the importance of the community of the theological campus as not only a "disengaged" people that intentionally set themselves apart, but also as committed to purposefully reengaging with the culture from the Christian worldview of the campus. This is key in developing students' ability to proclaim their faith, and the responses throughout the interviews were telling as to the importance of purposeful reengagement.

One student noted the common refrain that he entered college mostly holding beliefs as passed down from his family. The classroom forced him to cognitively struggle with their reality, but it was the active nature of the evangelistic emphasis of the campus[26] that forced him to own these beliefs and to be able to put words behind his faith. Another student explained how she had matured in her time on campus to where her story formed the background of her advice to others. This is good, but she demonstrated real maturity as she said that she was now able to "Take people along the same process where [she]'s been," while leading them to what she has learned without specifically referencing her experiences. Regarding this, she said, "God's story in their life is more important than my story in their life."

Learning to Fail

It was also telling to hear students explain opportunities where they shared their faith and did not always feel successful. Several students described these as opportunities to "fail and learn." The supportive atmosphere of the theological campus followed these students into a broad array of off-campus ministry opportunities, including traveling ministry teams, campus leadership, and summer internships. One student described just such an experience as she worked with unreached people groups in Russia during a summer internship. She described this time as an "opportunity to fail and to learn to depend upon God." But this failure, as in other similar accounts,

---

25. And thankfully so, as according to Philo's statement where he says that exile is worse even than death, "not second to death, if truth gives its verdict, but rather a far heavier punishment, since death ends our troubles, but banishment is not the end but the beginning of other new misfortunes." Philo, *Vol. VI, 64*.

26. This student spoke specifically of the Pack Your Bags program, but samplings from other students could just as well include annual GO Trips, various ministry team experiences at TBCGS, and campus leadership roles for those included in this study.

Emerging Voices

was always buffered by an assurance that students would be supported by their campus community and that they would learn from these experiences.

Another student explained that his calling had solidified as he was able to better understand his experiences in light of God's story and to put it into words. Specifically, this student had struggled with his call early on in his freshman year, but now he had grown in confidence that he was in the place God has called him. Out of this newfound level of assurance in his "place with God," he shares his faith with a new confidence. His maturation from needing to "feel" called to where he had come to know God as more than a feeling changed how he spoke to others about his faith and gave him confidence in doing so.

All of these students discussed intentional re-engagement opportunities as confidence-building exercises. This is especially interesting when one takes into account the survey I proposed as I closed my time with these students. In summarizing all that we had discussed in several hours of conversation, I asked the students to rate their confidence in verbalizing their faith on a scale of one through ten, beginning with their first day on campus as a freshman up until currently. The responses ranged from one to five when students first stepped on campus. This would seem to mean that their confidence in their first days of theological education was low to medium at best. As they shared their current level of confidence, the responses trended upward to where almost all of them claimed a seven or an eight currently (see figure 8). It seems in the case of these students that theological education had done an effective job, at least when it came to building a confidence in proclaiming their faith.

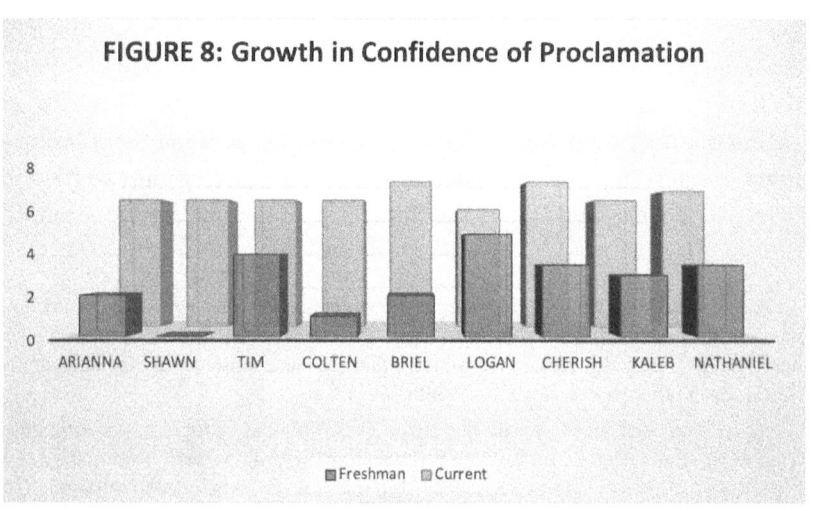

FIGURE 8: Growth in Confidence of Proclamation

Conclusion

As students expressed their lack of confidence prior to attending college, most of them did not specifically indicate newfound academic knowledge as the central factor for their increased confidence. Most of them noted opportunities to "practice" their proclamation and how this had helped them in learning to initiate theological conversations in their world. Certainly, this is not to say that students did not gain confidence from their increased theological acumen, but that they recognized the campus as more than an information center. Students recognized that their overall formation was at least equal to the opportunity to sharpen their intellectual grasp of the faith.

Overall, the exilic lens seems to be a fitting metaphor through which to see the theological campus, as long as it is applied in philosophical structure and not in building an oppositional mindset within the student body. It must be understood as temporary rather than normative and with a hopeful, rather than a separatist, perspective. Approaching the theological campus as an exilic community through these limited boundaries will be helpful in preparing students to first discover the language of the Christian faith and second to learn to proclaim it in the twenty-first century.

9

Keep the Conversation Going

AFTER THE FINAL INTERVIEWS in this study had taken place, I encountered one of the participants on campus. As we were talking, she shared that she had enjoyed the process, especially how "free she felt" in sharing her faith experiences with others throughout the interviews. As we prepared to go our separate ways, I made the passing statement, "Let's keep the conversation going." Moments later I realized that was exactly what this study had revealed. Theological students are looking for faith conversation partners. Particularly in their studies, they want adults who will model best practices in engaging their culture. In the classroom we offer tools—theological, biblical, and practical—but in relationship we offer the opportunity to be a part of something beyond vocational training; we offer an invitation to a conversation, a call to a mission.

At the conclusion of this study there is much that we have learned and yet more that I hope will draw interest of others who will continue the conversation. As I said at the outset, it is my hope that this project will inspire a conversation on faith language, particularly on the theological campus that seeks to train emerging adults for vocational ministry. As we close the book on this project, let us take a minute to examine what we have learned and what demands further engagement.

Have We Answered the Question?

As a reminder, the underlying question behind this study was: How does interaction among students, faculty, and staff on a theological campus affect students' ability to develop the ability to verbalize their faith? In the following pages, we will attempt to review some of the cultural impact, the role of theological education in countering this, and examine the usefulness of the exilic metaphor in addressing these concerns.

The "Silencing" Effect of Secularism

It is evident in both existing research as well as in the interviews done for this project, that secularism has proven to be a pervasive force, including its effect on theological students. The Christian faith still holds the view that religious language is important, and yet the discussion above demonstrates that Christianity has lost confidence in its place in Western culture. Specifically, the NSYR demonstrated a lack of confidence in being able to put words to one's faith. As mentioned, this facet was apparent in the students I interviewed for this study, as they entered theological education with a low level of confidence when it came to proclaiming their faith. Students in this study did however demonstrate certain distinctions from the sample of the NSYR, namely that their language did not exhibit the same therapeutic tone as the average emerging adult.[1] Overall, it can be concluded that emerging adults—even those called into vocational ministry—do display the effects of a secular culture that is consistent both with the philosophical dichotomy of secularism, and with the sociological evidence of the effects of such a culture.

It is also notable that, although some demonstrated a level of confidence proclaiming their faith previously, almost every student demonstrated an increase in confidence, especially in their ability to proclaim it through sound theology. The emphasis of the students interviewed focused mostly on experiences outside the classroom, but it was evident that understanding gained in the classroom had provided a newfound level of self-assurance. This seems to suggest that the classroom is foundational, but that this formation is incomplete until it is integrated beyond the classroom. In

---

1. Smith identified a pervasive "therapeutic" tone in the interviews conducted for the NSYR that was "centrally about feeling good, happy, secure, at peace. It is about attaining subjective well-being, being able to resolve problems, and getting along amiably with other people." This language is what led Smith to characterize young peoples' view of God as combination "Divine Butler" and "Cosmic Therapist," meaning that, "he is always on call, takes care of any problems that arise, professionally helps his people feel better about themselves, and does not become too personally involved in the process." Smith, *Soul Searching*, 164–65.

this way, students demonstrated a point made by A. N. Williams, Professor of Divinity at the University of Cambridge and Fellow of Corpus Christi College, when he said, "We do not speak in order that others will be persuaded; we speak because we have been transformed."[2] This sort of transformation was apparent in the students I interviewed. The silencing effect of secularism had been lifted, and they had authentic encounters with God and understood them more fully in conversation with adult mentors. These encounters, as described by students, have enhanced their understanding of God and have given them a confidence that faith language has a place in everyday conversation.

The predominance of experiences shared by students focused on opportunities to put the principles they were learning into action. Students commonly referred to this as having the opportunity to "practice" what they were learning in the classroom and throughout the campus community. Students emphasized the ability to "fail" and to learn from their experience in a "safe" environment. It can be assumed from these statements that students had not previously felt "at home" integrating their faith beyond environments deemed appropriate by secular society. By providing the educational foundation, the integrated culture, and the opportunity to proclaim their faith across different environments, students found their message to be germane and grew in confidence.

The Integrative Campus

Each student in the study, although coming from a wide variety of backgrounds, noted significant growth in confidence during their time on campus. It might be natural to assume this as mostly due to the students' focused theological education in their time at college, and presumably this was a factor. However, the consistent theme throughout the interviews was that the opportunity presented by everyday engagement on campus was perhaps even more formational than the educational component. Specifically, students noted that they had discovered a place where their faith and

---

2. Williams, "Mystical Theology Redux," 69. This quote was originally taken from Michael Pasquarello III, who emphasizes the point that this sort of formation causes one to speak, to proclaim: "Therefore, the more we are *con*-formed to God by divine wisdom, the more we will know him, and the more we know him, the more we will be drawn to him in love, and the more we are drawn to him in love, *the more we will speak and act in union with the incarnate Word*, who is both our way and our goal." Pasquarello, *We Speak Because Was Have First Been Spoken*, 13, emphasis added.

its holistic integration was encouraged, many of them noting this as a new experience. Although it is possible that further investigation would uncover deeper weight placed upon educational training, their experiences highlight that an integrative college experience contributed much to their ability to verbalize their faith. The general consensus seemed to be that the holistic faith integration of the campus community had done more for their confidence than the rudimentary learning of the vocabulary and its theological application.

The emphasis on the holistic influence of the campus suggests that the integrative approach is as important as ever in preparing young people for vocational ministry. However, it also reveals something more for a campus hoping to form students in conversational faith. Taylor critiques the traditional apologetic approach apparent in a large sampling of curriculum as "a less theologically elaborate faith" that succumbs to the very presuppositions of the secular worldview it counters.[3] Instead, this study suggests that the role of the theological campus must be to train students in a different sort of apologetics, one that seeks to be conversant with rather than against contemporary culture.

This sort of apologetic encourages conversation, as opposed to shutting it down. The role of the theological campus, then, is to be integrative in its approach not only to establish the place of Christian faith in a secular culture, but also to demonstrate the ability to interact outside of faith communities without losing the ability to maintain intelligent discourse.

This "new apologetic" needs to continue to develop in light of the culture in which contemporary emerging adults live, not that of past generations. Specifically, it would be helpful to see this approach applied to the integrational model of higher education. As the integrational model encourages holistic and propositional discourse, this would seem a natural fit, especially seen in light of the influence of conversational Christianity noted above and its evidence in the devoted youth from the NSYR.

---

3. Taylor, *A Secular Age*, 225. James K.A. Smith summarizes Taylor's thoughts: "What we get in the name of 'Christian' defenses of transcendence, then, is 'a less theologically elaborate faith' that, ironically, paves the way for exclusive humanism. God is reduced to a Creator and religion is reduced to morality. The 'deism' of providential deism bears many marks of the 'theism' that is often defended in contemporary apologetics. The particularities of specifically *Christian* belief are diminished to try to secure a more generic deity—as if saving *some* sort of transcendence will suffice." Smith, *How (Not) to be Secular*, 51.

Emerging Voices

The Exilic Campus Community

It would seem that students in this study demonstrate some level of exilic identity based upon the pervasive influence of the culture in which they live.[4] However, it would also be appropriate to say that none of them would self-identify this way. Although the exilic metaphor for the theological campus is helpful, it seems that students in this study identify more clearly in the image of second or third generation exiles. By this, I mean that today's emerging adult largely operates in a Christian culture that has already at least partially succumbed to the temptation of cultural syncretism,[5] and the influence of the predominant culture is not always altogether clear until one is presented with the Christian alternative.

For this reason it is helpful to search for corollary ministry models that envision a way forward, and refuse to see themselves as inconsequential to the culture around them.[6] The missional church model presents an approach to ministry that would seem to encourage this level of engagement[7] which, combined with the communal participation evident in a culture of creativity[8] and the conversational approach to Christianity,[9] would seem well suited to equip young ministers for effective engagement in a foreign culture.

---

4. Brueggemann notes two pertinent points of contact between the ancient exile and the contemporary church: "(1) loss of a structured, reliable 'world' where (2) treasured symbols of meaning are mocked and dismissed." Brueggemann, *Cadences of Home*, 2.

5. Brueggemann points out just such an occasion for Israel in the Hellenistic period: "The Maccabean period offers us an example of Jewish boys who were embarrassed about their circumcision and who tried to 'pass.'" Brueggemann, *Cadences of Home*, 104.

6. James Davison Hunter notes the established approaches of different Christian traditions: "the evangelical approach as 'defense against' the culture, the liberal approach as 'relevance to' the culture, and the Anabaptist approach as 'purity from' the culture." Hunter, *To Change the World*, 213.

7. Craig Van Gelder identifies the main themes of the missional church as: (1) God is a missionary God who sends the church in to the world; (2) God's mission in the world is related to the reign (kingdom) of God; (3) The missional church is an incarnational (versus an attractional) ministry sent to engage a postmodern, post-Christendom, globalized context; (4) The internal life of the missional church focuses on every believer living as a disciple engaging in mission. Van Gelder and Zscheile, *The Missional Church in Perspective*, 4.

8. Sir Ken Robinson addresses this in Robinson, *Out of Our Minds*, 182: (1) Creativity is not a purely personal process; (2) Creativity is a dynamic process and can involve many different areas of expertise; (3) Creativity is incremental; (4) Cultural change is not linear and smooth; (5) Cultural change is not strictly logical.

9. Dean, *Almost Christian*, 135–37; 144–46.

The theological campus would also do well to examine communal models from other faith communities to apply to its own communal approach.[10] Some of these models might include radical orthodoxy,[11] the missional church,[12] or even the contemporary pietistic movement.[13]

Continuing the Conversation

Contemporary Western culture is defined as much by *what it is no longer* than what it is. We live in a "post" culture. Although secularism was chosen as a focus for this project, due to its direct effect upon the verbalization of faith, studies beyond the secular influence on language are necessary to fully unpack the problem. Postmodernism and the church's ministry to emerging generations have been jointly dealt with in previous publications,[14] but more could be done to specifically address the reclamation of the Christian language in light of twenty-first century Western culture, specifically regarding emerging adulthood.

Similarly, emerging adults today have been largely shaped by the technology in their hands. In this, the theological campus must not only recognize the resulting challenges to communication, but also how this has affected faith proclamation directly. The theological campus who recognizes that screens disciple stands with students who seek to learn how to reshape their lives as God's image bearers and have the potential to speak hope to their peers through their experience. It seems clear that today's students are

---

10. I am reminded of a book assigned to me in graduate school that described innovation as a coming together of divergent views. The overall premise of the book is that often the most innovative ideas come from seemingly non-related fields of study. By looking to other Christian communities and, in fact, other communities of many kinds, the theological campus might find innovative ways of building community. Razeghi. *the riddle*. Similarly, in Epstein. *Range*.

11. See *Radical Orthodoxy*, ed. by Milbank et al.; Smith. *Introducing Radical Orthodoxy*.

12. The Missional Church movement has been widely addressed in recent years, but some samples of useful resources include Frost and Hirsch, *The Shaping of Things to Come*; Hirsch, *The Forgotten Ways*; Woodward and White, *The Church as Movement*, and Gibbs. *The Rebirth of the Church*

13. This is not as wide spread of a model as the previously mentioned movements, but for an introduction see Gehrz and Pattie, *The Pietist Option*. This text serves chiefly as a call back to the origins of Pietism, as outlined in Spener. *Pia Desideria*.

14. See, for instance, Jones, *Postmodern Youth Ministry*, and Beckwith, *Postmodern Children's Ministry*.

asking for the wisdom of their elders in how to handle the power they have been given, and it is imperative that the theological campus lead the way in this discussion. We are, after all, training the students that will become the pastors of tomorrow, helping the church to deal with these very issues.

In addition to the prevalent influence of the culture, the church's role must be considered. In the Western church's attempt at relativity, it is important to question what might have been lost. It would be foolish to think that culture alone is responsible for the concerns addressed in this paper. An examination of the church's role and response would be helpful in this discussion.[15]

Regarding the exilic lens, further studies demonstrating this metaphor at work in second, third, and generations beyond would be helpful as Christianity continues to be pushed to the margins of Western culture. Especially useful would be studies regarding the reclamation of language, specifically faith proclamation, in communities which have largely lost this identifying feature.

Lastly, it would be helpful to examine this issue through the lens of non-ministry students in measuring the impact of the theological campus. In the same vein, a broader examination of Christian colleges and liberal arts universities would be helpful. Namely, it could be examined whether the integration model proves useful in these settings, and whether the exilic lens might be helpful.

Conclusion

It is apparent from this study that emerging adults entering the theological campus seek an integrative environment which will help them assimilate their faith into their studies and to better prepare them for vocational ministry. The theological campus provides a suitable environment for this kind of development, however, only when it recognizes that much of this development takes place as an extension of the classroom. The theological campus must employ an integrative approach to education alongside of intentional mentoring such as Bonhoeffer's "place sharing" philosophy shared previously. It is this sort of community,[16] one recognizes the potential in

---

15. Helpful resources in this discussion would be Gilkey. *Naming the Whirlwind*, and Kinnaman. *You Lost Me*.

16. Andrew Root notes that Bonhoeffer's philosophy on ministering to emerging generations was that they are taken into community "not through rational consent

others and sees the opportunity to serve and to pour into emerging generations[17] with which today's students most seem to identify. Proposals such as the exilic model and others should be critically engaged as the theological campus continues to address the challenges of integrated Christian higher education in the twenty-first century. With this commitment to integrative biblical training, communal commitment and cooperative creativity, the theological campus is well suited to equip emerging generations to proclaim their faith well in the world in which they live.

---

but through person's acting with and for the child's person." Root, *Bonhoeffer As Youth Worker*, 50.

17. Green sees this in *Stellvertretung*: "it is the Christological basis of that 'being with one another' . . . and 'active being for one another' . . . the sociality of Christ in his love for humanity personifies and creates the sociality of the new humanity." Green, *Bonhoeffer: A Theology of Sociality*, 58.

Bibliography

Alexander, Philip. "Jewish Nationalism from Judah the Macabee to Judah the Prince and the Problem of 'Continuing Exile.'" In *Exile: A Conversation with N.T. Wright*, edited by James M. Scott, 137–62. Downers Grove, IL: InterVarsity Academic, 2017.

Andrew-Gee, Eric. "Your Smartphone Is Making You Stupid, Antisocial, and Unhealthy. So Why Can't You Put It Down?" *The Globe and Mail*, January 6, 2018, https://www.theglobeandmail.com/technology/your-smartphone-is-making-you-stupid/article37511900/.

Arnett, Jeffrey Jensen. *Emerging Adulthood: The Winding Road from the Late Teens Through the Twenties.* 2nd ed. New York: Oxford University Press, 2014.

Augustine, *Confessions*. Translated by Albert C. Outler. 397–98. Reprint, Barnes & Noble Classics. New York: Barnes & Noble, 2007.

Balzer, Carey L. "Leaving A Mark: The Role of Faculty in University-Wide Spiritual Formation." In *Building A Culture of Faith: University-Wide Partnerships for Spiritual Formation*, edited by Cary Balzer and Rod Reed, 63–77. Abilene, TX: Abilene Christian University Press, 2012.

Balzer, Carey L., and Rod Reed, eds. *Building A Culture of Faith: University-Wide Partnerships for Spiritual Formation.* Abilene, TX: Abilene Christian University Press, 2012.

Bauer, Walter, et al., eds. *A Greek-English Lexicon of the New Testament and Other Early Christian Literature.* Chicago: The University of Chicago Press, 1957.

Becker, Anne E. "Television, Disordered Eating, and Young Women in Fiji: Negotiating Body Image and Identity During Rapid Social Change," *Culture, Medicine and Psychiatry* 28, no. 4 (2004) 533–59.

Berger, Peter. *Facing Up to Modernity: Excursions in Society, Politics, and Religion.* New York: Basic, 1977.

———. *The Sacred Canopy.* New York: Anchor, 1969.

Bergler, Thomas E. *The Juvenilization of American Christianity.* Grand Rapids: Eerdmans, 2012.

Bethge, Eberhard. *Dietrich Bonhoeffer: A Biography.* Minneapolis: Fortress, 2000.

Bird, Michael F. "Jesus and the Continuing Exile of Israel in the Writings of N.T. Wright." *Journal for the Study of the Historical Jesus* 13, no. 2/3 (May 2015) 209–31.

Bonhoeffer, Dietrich. *Dietrich Bonhoeffer Works, Volume 1: Sanctorum Communio: A Theological Study of the Sociology of the Church.* Minneapolis: Fortress, 2005.

———. *Dietrich Bonhoeffer Works, Volume 4: Discipleship.* Minneapolis: Fortress Press, 2005.

Bibliography

———. *Dietrich Bonhoeffer Works, Volume 5: Life Together and Prayerbook of the Bible.* Minneapolis: Fortress, 2005.

Bosanquet, Mary. *The Life and Death of Dietrich Bonhoeffer.* New York: Harper & Row, Publishers, 1968.

Brueggemann, Walter. *Cadences of Home: Preaching Among Exiles.* Louisville: Westminster John Knox, 1997.

———. *The Creative Word: Canon as a Model for Biblical Education.* Philadelphia: Fortress, 1982.

———. "Praise to God Is the End of Wisdom: What Is the Beginning?" *Journal for Preachers* 12, no. 3 (Easter 1989) 30–40.

———. "Wright on Exile: A Response." In *Exile: A Conversation with N.T. Wright*, edited by James M. Scott, 83–92. Downers Grove, IL: InterVarsity Academic, 2017.

Bryan, Steven M. "Jesus and Israel's Eschatological Constitution." In *Handbook for the Study of the Historical Jesus*, edited by T. Holmen and S. E Porter, 3 2835–53. 4 vols. Leiden: Brill, 2004.

Carlson, Kent, and Mike Leuken. *Renovation of the Church: What Happens When A Seeker Church Discovers Spiritual Formation.* Downers Grove, IL: IVP, 2011.

Carpenter, Joel A. "The Mission of Scholarship in the New Millennium." In *Faithful Learning and the Scholarly Vocation*, edited by Douglas V. Henry and Bob R. Agee, 62–74. Grand Rapids: Eerdmans, 2003.

Christakis, Nicholas A., and James H. Fowler. *Connected: The Surprising Power of Our Social Networks and How They Shape Our Lives.* New York: Little, Brown, 2009.

Clark, Chap. *Adoptive Church: Creating an Environment Where Emerging Generations Belong.* Grand Rapids: Baker Academic, 2018.

———. *Adoptive Youth Ministry: Integrating Emerging Generations in the Family of Faith.* Grand Rapids: Baker Academic, 2016.

———. *Hurt 2.0: Inside the World of Today's Teenagers.* Grand Rapids: Baker Academic, 2011.

Clark, Chap, ed. *Youth Ministry in the Twenty-First Century: Five Views.* Grand Rapids: Baker Academic, 2015.

Clarke, Erskine, ed. *Exilic Preaching: Testimony for Christian Exiles in an Increasingly Hostile Culture.* Harrisburg, PA: Trinity, 1998.

Coyne, Sarah M. "Pretty as a Princess: Longitudinal Effects of Engagement with Disney Princesses on Gender Stereotypes. Body Esteem, and Prosocial Behavior in Children." *Child Development* 87, no. 6 (2016) 1909–25.

Crawford Cheryl A., and Daniel Gillooley. "Sticky Faith Turns 30." Lecture, 2018 Association of Youth Ministry Educators Annual Conference, Association of Youth Ministry Educators, St. Louis, MO, October 28, 2018.

Dean, Kenda Creasy. *Almost Christian: What the Faith of Our Teenagers is Telling the American Church.* New York: Oxford University Press, 2010.

Dean, Kenda Creasy, et al. *Delighted: What Teenagers Are Teaching the Church About Joy.* Grand Rapids: Eerdmans, 2020.

Detweiler, Craig. *Selfies: Searching for the Image of God in a Digital Age.* Grand Rapids: Brazos, 2018.

Doll, Jen. "On the Importance of Having Superheroes." *The Atlantic.* May 7, 2012. https://www.theatlantic.com/entertainment/archive/2012/05/importance-having-superheroes/328461/.

Dunn, Richard R. *Shaping the Journey of Emerging Adults: Life-Giving Rhythms for Spiritual Transformation.* Downers Grove, IL: InterVarsity, 2012.

Bibliography

Eadicicco, Lisa. "Americans Check Their Phone 8 Billion Times a Day." *TIME*, December 15, 2015. https://time.com/4147614/smartphone-usage-us-2015/.

Elkind, David. *A Sympathetic Understanding of the Child: Birth to Sixteen*. Needham Heights, MA: Allyn & Bacon, 1994.

Epstein, David. *Range: Why Generalists Triumph in a Specialized World*. New York: Riverhead Books, 2019.

Erickson, Erik H. *Identity: Youth and Crisis*. New York: Norton, 1968.

Espinoza, Chip, et al. *Managing the Millennials: Discover the Core Competencies for Managing Today's Workforce*. Hoboken, NJ: John Wiley & Sons, 2010.

Evans, C. Stephen. "The Calling of the Christian Scholar-Teacher." In *Faithful Learning and the Scholarly Vocation*, edited by Douglas V. Henry and Bob R. Agee, 26–49. Grand Rapids: Eerdmans, 2003.

Fioretti, Chiara, et al. "The Role of the Listener on the Emotional Valence of Personal Memories in Emerging Adulthood." *Journal of Adult Development* 24, no. 4 (December 2017) 252–62.

Freitas, Donna. *The Happiness Effect: How Social Media Is Driving a Generation to Appear Perfect at Any Cost*. New York: Oxford University Press, 2017.

Frost, Michael. *Exiles: Living Missionally in a Post-Christian Culture*. Peabody, MA: Hendrickson, 2006.

Frost, Michael, and Alan Hirsch. *The Shaping of Things to Come: Innovation and Mission for the 21st Century Church*. Peabody, MA: Hendrickson, 2003.

Gay, Craig M. *Modern Technology and the Human Future: A Christian Appraisal*. Downers Grove, IL: InterVarsity Academic, 2018.

Gehrz, Christopher, and Mark Pattie III. *The Pietist Option: Hope for the Renewal of Christianity*. Downers Grove, IL: InterVarsity Academic, 2017.

Gen Z: The Culture, Beliefs and Motivations Shaping the Next Generation. Barna Research Group and Impact 360 Institute, 2018.

Gibbs, Eddie. *The Rebirth of the Church: Applying Paul's Vision for Ministry in Our Post-Christian World*. Grand Rapids, MI: Baker Academic, 2013.

Gilkey, Langdon. *Naming the Whirlwind: The Renewal of God-Language*. Indianapolis, IN: Bobbs-Merrill, 1976.

Gladwell, Malcolm. "Small Change: Why the Revolution Will Not Be Tweeted." *The New Yorker*, October 4, 2010. http://www.newyorker.com/magazine/2010/10/04/small-change-3.

Glanzer, Perry L. "Who Are We to Form Students?: The Importance of Remembering Who We Are." In *Building A Culture of Faith: University-Wide Partnerships for Spiritual Formation*, edited by Cary Balzer and Rod Reed, 109–23. Abilene, TX: Abilene Christian University Press, 2012.

Gramlich, John. "Young Americans Are Less Trusting of Other People—and Key Institutions—Than Their Elders." Pew Research Group, August 6, 2019. https://www.pewresearch.org/fact-tank/2019/08/06/young-americans-are-less-trusting-of-other-people-and-key-institutions-than-their-elders/.

Green, Clifford J. *Bonhoeffer: A Theology of Sociality*, Revised, subsequent ed. Grand Rapids: Eerdmans, 1999.

Greenway, Tyler S., et al. "Getting Warmer: What Growing Young Research on the Importance of Relational Warmth Reveals About Churches' Self-Assessment with Implications for Future Youth Ministry Practitioners." *Journal of Youth Ministry* 16, no. 3 (Fall 2018) 86–105.

Bibliography

Guinness, Os. *Fool's Talk: Recovering the Lost Art of Christian Persuasion.* Downers Grove, IL: InterVarsity, 2015.

Hampton, Keith, et. al. "Social Media and the 'Spiral of Silence.'" Pew Research Center's Internet & American Life Project, August 26, 2014. http://www.pewinternet.org/2014/08/26/social-media-and-the-spiral-of-silence.

Hatch, Nathan O. *The Democratization of American Christianity.* New York: Oxford University Press, 1991.

Hauerwas, Stanley. "Carving Stone: Learning to Speak Christian." Lecture, 2007 Princeton Lectures on Youth, Church, and Culture, Princeton Theological Seminary, Princeton, NJ, April 30, 2007.

———. *Working With Words: On Learning to Speak Christian.* Eugene, OR: Cascade, 2011.

Hauerwas, Stanley, and William H. Willimon. *Resident Aliens: Life in the Christian Colony.* Nashville: Abingdon, 1989.

Henry, Douglas V., and Bob R. Agee, eds. *Faithful Learning and the Christian Scholarly Vocation.* Grand Rapids: Eerdmans, 2003.

Hirsch, Alan. *The Forgotten Ways: Reactivating Apostolic Movements.* Grand Rapids: Brazos, 2016

Houtman, Dick, and Stef Aupers. "The Spiritual Turn and the Decline of Tradition: The Spread of Post-Christian Spirituality in 14 Western Countries, 1981–2000." *Journal for the Scientific Study of Religion* 46, no. 3 (2007) 305–20.

Hunter, James Davison. *To Change the World: The Irony, Tragedy, and Possibility of Christianity in the Late Modern World.* New York: Oxford University Press, 2010.

Jacobsen, Douglas, and Rhonda Hustedt Jacobsen. *Scholarship & Christian Faith: Enlarging the Conversation.* New York: Oxford University Press, 2004.

Jones, L. Gregory, and Stephanie Paulsen. *The Scope of Our Art: The Vocation of the Theological Teacher.* Grand Rapids: Eerdmans, 2002.

Jones, Stanton L., and Richard E. Butman, *Modern Psychotherapies: A Comprehensive Christian Appraisal.* 2nd ed. Downers Grove, IL: InterVarsity Academic, 2011.

Josefsson, Ulrik. "The Role of Pentecostalism in Community Transformation." Presentation for the World Alliance for Pentecostal Theological Education Affinity Group at the Pentecostal World Conference, Calgary, AB, CA, August 28, 2019.

Ketcham, Sharon Galgay. *Reciprocal Church: Becoming A Community Where Faith Flourishes Beyond High School.* Downers Grove, IL: InterVarsity, 2018.

Kieffer, Jörn. "Not All Gloom and Doom: Positive Interpretations of Exile and Diaspora in the Hebrew Bible and Early Judaism." In *Exile: A Conversation with N.T. Wright*, edited by James M. Scott, 119–34. Downers Grove, IL: InterVarsity Academic, 2017.

Kimball, Dan. *They Like Jesus But Not the Church: Insights from Emerging Generations.* Grand Rapids, MI: Zondervan, 2007.

Kinnaman, David, and Mark Matlock. *Faith for Exiles: 5 Ways for a New Generation to Follow Jesus in Digital Babylon.* Grand Rapids, MI: Baker, 2019.

Kinnaman, David. *You Lost Me: Why Young Christians Are Leaving the Church . . . and Rethinking Faith.* Grand Rapids, MI: Baker, 2016.

Lefkowitz, Eva S., et al. "Communication with Best Friends About Sex-Related Topics During Emerging Adulthood." *Journal of Youth and Adolescence* 33, no. 4 (August 2004) 339–51.

Lindholm, Jennifer A. "Spirituality in the Academy: Reintegrating Our Lives and the Lives of Our Students." *About Campus* 12, no. 4 (September 2007) 10–17.

Bibliography

Linhart, Terry, ed. *Teaching the Next Generations: A Comprehensive Guide for Teaching Christian Formation.* Grand Rapids: Baker Academic, 2016.

Lukianoff, Greg, and Jonathan Haidt, *The Coddling of the American Mind: How Good Intentions and Bad Ideas Are Setting Up A Generation for Failure.* New York: Penguin, 2018.

Lyon, David. "Secularization and Sociology: The History of an Idea." *Fides Et Historia* 13, no. 2 (Spr 1981) 38–52.

Marshall, Paul, et al., eds. *Stained Glass.* Lanham, MD: University Press of America, 1989.

Metaxas, Eric. *Bonhoeffer: Pastor, Martyr, Prophet, Spy.* Nasville: Thomas Nelson, 2010.

Milbank, John, et al., eds. *Radical Orthodoxy.* New York: Routledge, 1999.

Molloy, Mark. "Facebook Addiction 'Activates Same Part of the Brain as Cocaine.'" *The Telegraph*, February 17, 2016, https://www.telegraph.co.uk/news/12161461/Facebook-addiction-activates-same-part-of-the-brain-as-cocaine.html.

Moltmann, Jürgen. *The Crucified God.* Minneapolis: Fortress, 2015.

Moore, R. Laurence. *Touchdown Jesus: The Mixing of Sacred and Secular in American History.* Louisville, KY: Westminster John Knox, 2003.

Murray, Stuart. *Post-Christendom: Church and Mission in a Strange New World.* 2nd ed. Eugene, OR: Cascade, 2018.

Nañez, Rick M. *Full Gospel, Fractured Minds?: A Call to Use God's Gift of Intellect* Grand Rapids: Zondervan, 2005.

Noll, Mark A. *The New Shape of World Christianity: How American Experience Reflects Global Faith.* Downers Grove, IL: InterVarsity Academic, 2009.

Palmer, Parker J. "Toward A Spirituality of Higher Education." In *Faithful Learning and the Christian Scholarly Vocation*, edited by Douglas V. Henry and Bob R. Agee, 75–86. Grand Rapids: Eerdmans, 2003.

Parker, James. "The Advice that Most 2020 Commencement Speakers Won't Give." *The Atlantic*, May 24, 2020. https://www.theatlantic.com/culture/archive/2020/05/the-advice-that-most-2020-commencement-speakers-wont-give/612040/.

Pascal, *Pensees.* Translated by W. F. Trotter. 1669. Reprint, Dover Thrift Editions. Minneapolis: Dover, 2018.

Pasquarello, Michael III. *We Speak Because Was Have First Been Spoken.* Grand Rapids: Eerdmans, 2009.

Pearcey, Nancy. *Total Truth: Liberating Christianity from its Cultural Captivity.* Wheaton, IL: Crossway, 2004.

Peterson, Eugene H. *A Long Obedience in the Same Direction: Discipleship in an Instant Society.* 2nd ed. Downers Grove, IL: InterVarsity, 2000.

Philo, *Volume VI: On Abraham. On Joseph. On Moses.* Translated by F. H. Colson. Reprint, Loeb Classical Library. Cambridge, MA: Harvard University Press, 1935.

Plantinga, Cornelius Jr., *Not the Way It's Supposed to Be: A Breviary of Sin.* Grand Rapids: Eerdmans, 1995.

Powell, Kara, and Chap Clark. *Sticky Faith: Everyday Ideas to Build Lasting Faith in Your Kids.* Grand Rapids: Zondervan, 2011.

Powell, Kara, et al. *Growing Young: 6 Essential Strategies to Help Young People Discover and Love Your Church.* Grand Rapids: Baker, 2016.

Powell, Kara, and Steven Argue. *Growing With: Every Parent's Guide to Helping Teenagers and Young Adults Thrive in Their Faith, Family, and Future.* Grand Rapids: Baker, 2019.

Razeghi, Andrew. *The Riddle: Where Ideas Come From and How to Have Better Ones.* San Francisco: Jossey Bass, 2008.

Bibliography

Reed, Rod. "Historical and Contemporary Approaches to Spiritual Formation in the University." In *Building A Culture of Faith: University-Wide Partnerships for Spiritual Formation*, edited by Cary Balzer and Rod Reed, 45–62. Abilene, TX: Abilene Christian University Press, 2012.

Reese, Susan. "Conversation Creates Culture: Student Development and Spiritual Formation in the Christian University." In *Building a Culture of Faith: University-Wide Partnerships for Spiritual Formation*, edited by Cary Balzer and Rod Reed, 155–64. Abilene, TX: Abilene Christian University Press, 2012.

Reinke, Tony. *12 Ways Your Phone is Changing You*. Wheaton, IL: Crossway, 2017.

Renner, Ben. "American Families Spend Just 37 Minutes of Quality Time Together Per Day, Survey Finds." *Study Finds*, March 21, 2018. https://www.studyfinds.org/american-families-spend-37-minutes-quality-time/.

Robinson, Ken. *Out of Our Minds: Learning to Be Creative*. Chichester, UK: Capstone, 2001.

Root, Andrew. *Bonhoeffer as Youth Worker: A Theological Vision for Discipleship and Life Together*. Grand Rapids: Baker Academic, 2014.

———. *Faith Formation in a Secular Age: Responding to the Church's Obsession with Youthfulness*. Ministry in a Secular Age. Grand Rapids: Baker Academic, 2017.

———. "Faith Formation in a Secular Age." *Word & World* 37, no. 2 (Spring 2017) 128–41.

Ross, Richard. "Youth Ministry in Thirds: To Accelerate the Development of Lifetime Faith." *Journal of Youth Ministry* 16, no. 2 (Spring 2017) 90–104.

Ryan, Richard M. and Edward L. Deci. "Self-Determination Theory and the Facilitation of Intrinsic Motivation, Social Development, and Well-Being." *American Psychologist* 55, no. 1 (January 2000) 68–78.

Salmela-Aro, Katarina, et al. "Personal Goals During Emerging Adulthood: A 10-Year Follow Up." *Journal of Adolescent Research* 22, no. 6 (November 2007) 690–715.

Sanders, E. P. *Jesus and Judaism*. London: SCM Press, 1985.

Sayers, Mark. *Disappearing Church: From Cultural Relevance to Gospel Resilience*. Chicago: Moody, 2016.

Schaeffer, Francis A. *Escape from Reason*. InterVarsity Classics. Downers Grove, IL: InterVarsity, 2007.

———. *The God Who is There*. 30th Anniversary ed. Downers Grove, IL: InterVarsity, 1998.

Schlingensiepen, Ferdinand. *Dietrich Bonhoeffer 1906–1945: Martyr, Thinker, Man of Resistance*. Edinburgh: T. & T. Clark, 2010.

Scott, James M, ed. *Exile: A Conversation with N.T. Wright*. Downers Grove, IL: InterVarsity Academic, 2017.

Seemiller, Corey, and Meghan Grace. *Generation Z Goes to College*. San Francisco: Jossey-Bass, 2016.

Seidman, Irving. *Interviewing as Qualitative Research: A Guide for Researchers in Education & the Social Sciences*. 4th ed. New York: Teachers College Press, 2013.

Setran, David P., and Chris A. Kiesling. *Spiritual Formation in Emerging Adulthood: A Practical Theology for College and Young Adult Ministry*. Grand Rapids: Baker Academic, 2013.

Shirky, Clay. *Here Comes Everybody*. New York: Penguin, 2008.

Sire, James W. *Naming the Elephant: Worldview as a Concept*. Downers Grove, IL: InterVarsity Academic, 2004.

Bibliography

———. *The Universe Next Door: A Basic Worldview Catalog.* 5th ed. Downers Grove, IL: InterVarsity Academic, 2009.

Smith, Christian. *Lost in Transition: The Dark Side of Emerging Adulthood.* New York: Oxford University Press, 2011.

———. *Soul Searching: The Religious Lives of American Teenagers.* New York: Oxford University Press, 2005.

———. *Souls in Transition: The Religious and Spiritual Lives of Emerging Adults.* New York: Oxford University Press, 2009.

Smith, David I., and James K. A. Smith, eds. *Teaching and Christian Practices: Reshaping Faith & Learning.* Grand Rapids: Eerdmans, 2011.

Smith, James K. A. *How (Not) to be Secular: Reading Charles Taylor.* Grand Rapids: Eerdmans, 2014.

———. *Introducing Radical Orthodoxy: Mapping a Post-secular Theology.* Grand Rapids: Baker Academic, 2004.

———. *Who's Afraid of Postmodernism?: Taking Derrida, Lyotard, and Foucault to Church.* Grand Rapids: Baker Academic, 2006.

———. *You Are What You Love: The Spiritual Power of Habit.* Grand Rapids: Brazos, 2016.

Spener, Philip Jacob. *Pia Desideria.* Translated by Theodore G. Tappert. 1964. Philadelphia: Fortress, 2001.

Stein, Stephen J. *Communities of Dissent: A History of Alternative Religions in America.* New York: Oxford University Press, 2003.

Stewart, James. "Facebook Has 50 Minutes of Your Time Each Day. It Wants More." *The New York Times,* May 5, 2016. https://www.nytimes.com/2016/05/06/business/facebook-bends-the-rules-of-audience-engagement-to-its-advantage.html.

Swinton, John. *From Bedlam to Shalom: Towards a Practical Theology of Human Nature, Interpersonal Relationships and Mental Health Care.* Bern, Switzerland: Peter Lang, 2000.

Taleb, Nassim Nicholas. *Antifragile: Things That Gain from Disorder.* New York: Random House, 2014.

Taylor, Charles. *A Secular Age.* Cambridge, MA: The Belknap Press of Harvard University Press, 2007.

Thompson, Clive. *Smarter Than You Think: How Technology is Changing Our Minds for the Better.* New York: Penguin, 2014.

Tillich, Paul. *Dynamics of Faith.* New York: HarperCollins, 2001.

Turkle, Sherry. *Reclaiming Conversation: The Power of Talk in a Digital Age.* New York: Penguin, 2015.

Turkle-Willard, Rebecca Ellen. "The Irrelevant Opposition: Reference Groups in the Formation of Political Attitudes Among Partisan College Students." Undergraduate diss., Harvard College, 2014.

Twenge, Jean M. *iGen: Why Today's Super-Connected Kids Are Growing Up Less Rebellious, More Tolerant, Less Happy—and Completely Unprepared for Adulthood.* New York: Atria, 2017.

Van Dijck, Jose. *The Culture of Connectivity: A Critical History of Social Media.* New York: Oxford University Press, 2013.

Van Gelder, Craig, and Dwight J. Zscheile. *The Missional Church in Perspective: Mapping Trends and Shaping the Conversation.* Grand Rapids: Baker Academic, 2011.

Bibliography

Van Gennep, Arnold. *The Rites of Passage*. Translated by Monika B. Vizedom and Gabrielle L. Caffe. Chicago: University of Chicago Press, 1960.

Volf, Miroslav. *Exclusion and Embrace*. Nashville: Abingdon, 1996.

Wadell, Paul J. "Teaching as a Ministry of Hope." In *The Scope of Our Art: The Vocation of the Theological Teacher*, edited by L. Gregory Jones and Stephanie Paulsen, 120–34. Grand Rapids, MI: Eerdmans, 2002.

Walker-Rettberg, Jill. *Seeing Ourselves Through Technology: How We Use Selfies, Blogs, and Wearable Devices to See and Shape Ourselves*. London: Palgrave Macmillan, 2014.

Webber, Robert E. *The Younger Evangelicals: Facing the Challenges of the New World*. Grand Rapids: Baker, 2002.

White, James Emery. *Meet Generation Z: Understanding and Reaching the New Post-Christian World*. Grand Rapids: Baker, 2017.

Wilken, Robert. *The Spirit of Early Christian Thought: Seeking the Face of God*. New Haven, CT: Yale University Press, 2003.

Williams, A. N. "Mystical Theology Redux: The Pattern of Aquinas' *Summa Theologiae*." *Modern Theology* 13, no. 1 (Jan. 1997) 69.

Willimon, William H. "Postmodern Preaching: Learning to Love the Thickness of the Text." In *Exilic Preaching: Testimony for Christian Exiles in an Increasingly Hostile Culture,* edited by Erskine Clarke, 108–16. Harrisburg, PA: Trinity, 1998.

Wind, Renate. *Dietrich Bonhoeffer: A Spoke in the Wheel* Trans. by John Bowden. Grand Rapids: Eerdmans, 1992.

Wodak, Ruth. "Language, Power, and Identity." *Language Teaching* 45, no. 2 (Apr 2012) 215–33.

Wolters, Albert M. *Creation Regained: Biblical Basics for a Reformational Worldview*. Grand Rapids: Eerdmans, 1985.

———. "On the Idea of Worldview and Its Relation to Philosophy." In *Stained Glass*, edited by Paul Marshall, Sander Griffioen, and Richard J. Mouw, 14–26. Lanham, MD: University Press of America, 1989.

Woodward, J. R., and Dan White, Jr. *The Church as Movement: Starting and Sustaining Missional-Incarnational Communities*. Downers Grove, IL: InterVarsity, 2016

Wright, N. T. *Jesus and the Victory of God*. Minneapolis: Fortress, 1997.

———. *Paul and the Faithfulness of God*. Minneapolis: Fortress, 2013.

———. "Yet the Sun Will Rise Again: Reflections on the Exile and Restoration in the Second Temple Judaism, Jesus, Paul, and the Church Today." In *Exile: A Conversation with N. T. Wright*, edited by James M. Scott, 19–80. Downers Grove, IL: InterVarsity Academic, 2017.

www.ingramcontent.com/pod-product-compliance
Lightning Source LLC
Chambersburg PA
CBHW072151160426
43197CB00012B/2335